Fighting the Good Fight

By Michael Dorn

LeRue Books
www.lrpnv.com

Copyright 2023, Michael Dorn

Fighting the Good Fight published by LeRue Books, an imprint of LeRue Press, LLC

Manufactured in the United States of America

All rights reserved. Except as permitted under U.S. Copyright Act of 1976, no part of this publication may be reproduced, distributed, or transmitted in any form or by any means, or stored in a database or retrieval system, without the prior written permission of the publisher.

LeRue Press, LLC
280 Greg Street #10
Reno, NV 89502
775.849.3814
Visit our website at www.Lrpnv.com.

ISBN-978-1-938814-47-1

Printed in the United States of America

Book Design by Adam Rice Creative
Editing by Carol Purroy

First Edition: (November 2023)
10 9 8 7 6 5 4 3 2 1

Dedication

For Liam, my son.

Table of Contents

Preface 1
Chapter 1 Growing Up 7
Chapter 2 Be All You Can Be.................................. 27
Chapter 3 On My Own 43
Chapter 4 Stepping Up to Bat 53
Chapter 5 My Family 65
Chapter 6 After Diagnosis (My M.S.-Multiple
    Sclerosis 71
Chapter 7 Where Do We Go From Here? 85
Chapter 8 Fight the Power...................................... 101
Chapter 9 Evolutionary Change 107
Chapter 10 Final Words (for now) 117
Epilogue.. 123
Acknowledgement... 127
My Playlist 129
About the Author 133

Preface

I'm sorry I wasn't the dad I needed to be for you. Everything I did, I did to make your life better. I wish I could have been like the other fathers. I wish I could have given you everything your heart wished for. I hope this book gives you insight to my struggle and the inner strength that I tried to call on each time I wanted to quit. There were a lot of those times. I did the best I could to be a responsible person, but sometimes my best wasn't good enough. I hope this memoir is good enough for you to know me.

I felt that I needed a reason for writing this book. I felt that I needed a justification or rationale for sitting here and giving testimony for the actions and directions my life has taken. I told Trina, my second stepmother, that I needed a title to give my motivation. I wanted it to be "Stepping up to bat: a father's story" to tell my story of my life with my family. Another idea for a title would be "M.S. and Me; my battle with a disease that boggles the mind, shakes the heart, and weakens the strong." For years I've had bits and pieces come and go. Some I'd write down and some I would just ponder, then let slip away. So much is going through my head as to the why, how, and when. I just want to tell my story. I'm not a writer, but I have a story to tell.

So, who is my target audience? I don't think I want to focus on that. I want to focus on you – Liam – as my audience. I am writing this for you. Why? I think it's because by the time you got to the age of understanding the world, I was diagnosed with Multiple Sclerosis, and my attitude has withered. I say "has," not "had" because that condition is still present. I have done you a disservice; this is my attempt to make amends. I'm told that I lecture a lot and rant often. I try to talk to you often, but sometimes when I get to see you after working all day, fatigue has kicked in and, with that, the mood swings start. It's not fair to you. Sometimes you just want to talk, but you know I'm tired, so you don't push the issue. Always my protector.

In this book, I'll talk about the major milestones that made me the man I am. Some of it will be authentic and some of it, my interpretation of reality. It's my perspective which allowed whatever it is to affect me. Some stuff will have factual data behind it. I know this because they were presented to me when I argued that it wasn't true.

What is a good length for an introduction? I'm thinking "You want to say something, but you don't want to say too much." Shout out to my grand-niece Alicia for inspiring me to write. I may not have the scenery in the background, but I have the desire.

All my life I have jotted down notes to myself about whatever I was feeling or observing in the moment. I want to add these "side notes" in this book to recapture the rationale for saying what needed to be said at the time. I have words, and those words are only as good as my readers' perception of them. I want to be understood.

> [Side Note 07/09/17] Originally, I wanted to write about being a man and manning up to my problems, because I thought that's what men do, and I knew about that, but I realize gender had nothing to do with it. My mom, your grandma, is the best example I know.

With my generation, the man was responsible for providing for the family; the breadwinner. Mom did it alone. She did whatever it took to keep us sheltered, clothed, and fed. She taught me how to drive a stick-shift (manual transmission) car. Mom was stern and when that didn't work, she'd whup me and explain why she did it. She didn't ask for respect, she let her actions earn it. She taught me to take responsibility for my actions. My mom was my role model for the man I am today. She is my strength. It's not about being a strong father or mother. It's about being a strong person and stepping up to the plate; taking responsibility; fighting against all odds. Not to win; just make it to the next day. That's all I'm trying to do; complete my mission for the day to make it to the next day. If I can't see tomorrow, I lose the desire for today. I'm writing to get a message to you. This is what drives me. Is this really worth someone reading? My focus shifts away from you, but I'll bring it back.

There are so many lessons I want to teach you, Liam. I feel as if I'm running out of time. What does that mean? I don't know. I keep waiting for the other shoe to drop. I keep thinking my cognition is going to fail me. I can't help but think I'm on borrowed time. *So little to do and so much time* (Willy Wonka). Scratch that. Reverse it.

Lesson number *whatever*…I'm not going to number these because I don't want to give them order, priority, or to denote value or importance. I never wanted you to settle. I never wanted you to be mediocre. It'd be easy to achieve mediocrity. You just need to breathe. To be good at something takes work. To be *great* takes work, talent, and luck. Remember, luck is when preparation meets opportunity. Strive to be great, then being good will come easy. But you need to put in the work.

[Side Note 07/22/18] It's funny how I want to blame "writer's block" on why I haven't been writing because I need to finish this. The truth is it's really hard to get writer's block when you're writing about your life. My past is what it is. I haven't been writing because I'm allowing my depression to turn this into a mountain and I'm getting tired of climbing.

I'm losing sight of the reason for this book. This is for you, Liam, my son. I want you to know what I've been through and am going through, not to give you an excuse to fail, but to inspire you to succeed. "Push Through."

Chapter 1
Growing up

In my earliest memories, I see a white lady, my Aunt Nina, whom I loved greatly. She was, in effect, my second mother. I stayed with her as a little kid in Killeen, Texas. She taught me what a coaster is. She explained to me that *gesundheit* means good health. She gave me a sense of culture and manners. I've not forgotten them. Aunt Nina, my uncle's wife, was Danish. Based on some of the older photos I saw at Grannie's house, she and my mom were close. It was Aunt Nina who named me. It is because of Aunt Nina that the idea of race never entered my world . . . until it did. It is because of Aunt Nina that I carry the lesson of treating people based on how they treat you, not because of how they look. To this day, I miss Aunt Nina.

Growing up in Texas, you learn quickly that there's a lot in a name. Not being a part of a family has haunted me since I was a child. I grew up the youngest of six. I was the only one with my last name. My mother and all my siblings had the same last name, from her first marriage, Scurlock. I wasn't so lucky. This was the introduction to my identity crisis. My grandmother, who structured much of my life and character, had a different last name from all of us, but her last name was the same as Aunt Nina and Uncle Alvin (aka Unkee) – Mills. I've always found comfort in their last name. I found strength in it. As much as I wanted to be a Scurlock, I would have rather been a Mills. Scurlock came from Mom's first husband, who I did not know at all, other than that he was the father of my oldest three siblings. Mills had a history that I could trace back to Tyler and Crockett, Texas, where Grannie grew up. I wanted to be anything other than a Dorn. And I didn't want to be alone.

Dorn was my dad's surname. The specifics as to how it became my surname weren't known to me until I was an adult. My dad wasn't around a lot. For the longest time, I thought he was both Bobbie's and my dad because she got most of his attention whenever he was around. As a child, what I knew of my dad was that he was married, with some stepsons. I went over to their house a few times, but we were not close. When I say close, I mean in the sense of being tight. We were close, proximity-wise; very close. They lived less than a mile from Grannie's house. In fact, they lived a couple of blocks from the corner store where Grannie and Mom would send us to get their cigarettes.

I cannot speak of my relationship with my dad without telling you about the man. Once I realized that Robert Dorn was my dad, I was in awe that I was the son of the man everyone in Midland knew. He owned this red car that he drove around town. I think it was an LTD. Everyone said, "There goes Reverend Rob's red ride." "Reverend," because he was a preacher and a pretty good Gospel singer. I thought that was the coolest thing. I wanted to be associated with the coolest man in Midland. I was his son. That should have been an automatic association, but it never happened.

Every once in a while, for Christmas, he would bring gifts to the house for Bobbie and me. When I was sixteen, I washed my sister Brenda's car in my mom's front yard because she was letting me drive it to the prom that night. I had a date, and Brenda had the coolest car in the family . . . the coolest one that I could use, that is. Although Robert had this really cool sportscar, he didn't offer it to me to drive. I digress. Anyway, while I was washing the car, Robert pulled up to the house with a girl around my age in the passenger seat. I knew she hung out with Cookie from the neighborhood. Robert introduced her as my half-sister. Come to find out, she was only a few months younger than I and lived a couple of blocks from where we lived. "Papa was a rolling stone.

Wherever he laid his hat was his home."[17] (The Temptations).

This was the first of many insights on Robert. I won't say he was a bad dad, but he wasn't good. I promised myself that I would not speak ill of your grandpa as long as he was a part of your life. The truth is, I hadn't spoken to Robert for a few years prior to your birth. When you were six-months old and your mother, you, and I were in Midland for a family reunion, I made a point to introduce you and your mother to him. We went by his job so he could get a look at y'all. He made no other effort to see you during that trip. It was never a secret where to find us in Midland; Grannie's address never changed from the day I was born. I would not make any more attempts to get him to be a grandfather to my child.

I guess he put as much effort in being your grandpa as he did to being my dad. This non-relationship has had a lasting effect on me. I just didn't realize it when I was a child. Thank God I had my mom's family.

Being the youngest of my siblings had its good and odd moments. I won't say "bad," just odd, because everything I went through with them made me the person I am. When it comes to my siblings, I'll introduce them in chronological order so it doesn't seem that I have a favorite, but we know I do. The six kids had four different fathers.

The first three were from my mom's marriage, which gave her the surname Scurlock. She never remarried. The last three were from three different fathers.

My oldest brother, Junior, was my hero. He was the strongest person I knew, except for Unkee. Junior was a smooth operator – a hustler. He was always into something. I saw him as more of an idol than a role model. He had a friend named Jim. As a kid, I always wanted to hang out with them. It wasn't suitable for someone that young to be exposed to some of the things he exposed me to. Junior was all about getting dressed up to go out. I'm recalling a house on Oak Street, near the boondocks. I tagged along with him while he worked. I remember his LPs: *Parliament, LTD, Skyy,* to name a few.

Junior was an artist – a phenomenal sketcher. He graduated from high school and went to Midland College. I thought he was going to be a huge success. Then there was the accident that sent a winch through the cabin of his work truck. It smashed half of his face. I couldn't recognize him when I went to see him in the hospital. He got a nice settlement from the accident, with which he bought a "mean" truck with a "sick" system. It was the "baddest" on the block.

His friend, Stoney, borrowed the truck and tried to smuggle drugs across the Mexican border.

Stoney got caught and the truck was impounded. Junior was a petty drug dealer. He sold weed while living in Mom's house. This led to a long life of drug use, being in and out of jail, being relatively homeless, and working labor jobs for cash. But that's his story – just know that he was the male influence in my life; good, bad, or indifferent.

Next up is Sandra, who shared a lot of Junior's characteristics, being that they were so close in age. Sandra was an attractive young lady and like Junior, she was a smooth operator. She had boyfriends, none of which I liked. Sandra and I never really bonded because we did not have a lot in common. The thing that Sandra had that I treasure is my niece. Sandra was the first to have kids and she had Kiss when I was 8 years old. I became an uncle. Kiss was my sidekick. I call her my First-Favorite niece.

Then there was Teddy, the sibling that scared me the most. I'll admit that I picked on him a lot as a kid, and he would scare the hell out of me chasing me around. I'm sure if he had caught me, he would have seriously hurt me. Talk about going from 0-to-100. He was also the reason I enjoyed motorcycles. He was responsible for getting me to school. We didn't live in the zone for the "good" school, so we used Grannie's address, but then had to work out how to get me to school. After school was out, I'd catch the bus and walk to Grannie's house. Back to Teddy... He made me wear a helmet whenever he gave me a ride to school – a simple act that elevated me. I didn't know of anyone else who got a ride to school on a motorcycle or wore a helmet.

Teddy was also the one who introduced me to comic books. This opened a whole new world for me. I learned some of my best words from comic books. I learned that *uncanny* is actually a word. I escaped reality in the pages of comic books. I was exposed to science fiction and wonderment as I lay there flipping through pages while listening to Michael Jackson's *Off the Wall* album. "She's Out of My Life[9]" was the best song ever. Comic books also turned out to be one of my worst addictions. I guess there are worse addictions, though.

Next up is Brenda. I had mixed emotions when it came to Brenda. I mostly envied her because her dad was a part of her life, and he made her a part of his. That envy would morph between desire and deep dislike. Albert Coutee, Brenda's dad, was a cool-ass man with some beautiful daughters. Brenda was the only girl that I ever called a bitch – the first and last. I was on the phone talking to someone and I told him, "She is such a bitch." Little did I know that she was eavesdropping on the other line. I made her cry and it bothered me. Whatever ill will I had toward Brenda, I didn't mean to make her cry.

The power of words is great and can do much harm.

Last, but not least, is Bobbie. I tried my best to emulate Bobbie. I wore my hat like her. I listened to Daryl Hall and John Oates like she did. The song "Kiss On My List"[7] comes to mind. She also introduced me to *The Rocky Horror Picture Show*. She brought Pop music and Rock N Roll into my life. Bobbie and I fought all the time, with her always winning. The most memorable time was when she choked me in Grannie's front yard while Mom was talking to the insurance man. She had this evil, maniacal look on her face. She choked me until I almost blacked out. It's something I've never forgotten or allowed her to forget.

I followed her everywhere. I went into the Army because she was in the Army. When she was diagnosed with M.S., I cried for quite a few days. Any time I had the opportunity to spend time with her, I did. Whether it was in Chicago, Arlington, or Baumholder, Germany. I could not have a bad time hanging with my sister, my idol, my role model, Bobbie.

My greatest influences, though, came from my cousins. Good, bad, or indifferent, a lot of who I am and how I think is based on growing up with them. First and foremost is Brad. Brad was more like a big brother than a cousin. My childhood became better when Brad entered my life. If I can't highlight anything from my childhood, in reference to Brad, I will tell you that he introduced me to Hip Hop. The first Hip Hop song I can honestly say that Brad opened my eyes to, would be "Planet Rock"[1] by Africa Bambaataa. But it wasn't just Hip Hop, it was music in general. We would connect the TV cable signal to the radio in Grannie's house so we could get a signal strong enough to get the radio station in Dallas on the weekends – Yvon Saint John and The Quiet Storm.

Brad was "the good." Well, mostly good. If that were the case, then my other two cousins would be classified as "the bad." I did a lot of my dirt with those two. They were like brothers to me, as well. I learned how to overcome my fears to do some really bad and sad crimes.

During my childhood, I drank a lot of alcohol; MD 20/20 was my drink. I also smoked a lot of weed. The weed came easy because Junior was dealing drugs while he stayed in Mom's house. We could steal from him and not worry about him telling on us. It was a win-win. I doubt he knew we were pinching off from his stash. He was a bad drug dealer, especially since he broke the #4 crack commandment…"never get high on your own supply." "Ten Crack Commandment"[16] by Notorious B.I.G. Regardless, we were all guilty of drug use and that only made things worse.

As we grew, we also grew apart. Brad was doing his high school track thing and getting into a serious relationship. The other two escalated their brazen thievery and drug use. They got jobs one summer at a neighborhood car wash. Having a job would keep the heat off of them because I know that Unkee and their mom were wondering where all the bikes, clothes, and electronic games came from. They needed legitimate jobs to have cover. They were hired, but I wasn't. Out of jealousy, I went to the Army recruiter's office and signed up. Yes, it was that simple and that petty. I didn't sign up out of some great desire to serve my country. I did it to get a job.

I cannot give you the specifics as to how it all came about, but Brad went back to San Diego and the other cousins were in and out of police custody. I don't know if it was a dream, but I have a vision of one of my cousins getting arrested in Grannie's front yard as I was being driven to the bus station to go to Fort Bliss (El Paso), Texas to start Basic Training. To be honest, it's all a fuzzy haze. In any case, I was no longer hanging with my cousins in Midland, Texas. I was on to my next life.

Grannie only had two children, my mom and her brother, my Unkee. Unkee was the younger sibling, but he was the patriarch of the family. If there was a need to get to anywhere in the country, we drove there. If there was driving to be done, 9 times out of 10, Unkee was behind the wheel. If something was broken, Unkee would fix it. Unkee was the quintessential man.

I know that Unkee was in the Army. I'm not sure if he fought in the Vietnam War. We never really talked about that. I know that later on he drove an 18-wheeler, hauling pipe for oil companies. I know that during the summer, when I was out of school, I would ride with him to different towns. Most of the time, it was on the way to Houston, where I'd stay with his family.

Unkee had gotten a divorce from my Aunt Nina and got married to Alma, who had three boys from a previous marriage. All I can tell you is that my time with Unkee's family taught me a lot. The three boys were Wayne (oldest), Cuda (my age), and Ballee (youngest). I can't be totally sure, but I think they lived in one of the wards of Houston; 4th or 5th. I know it was a poor neighborhood. Aunt Alma cooked red beans and rice almost every night. I didn't realize until I was older that this was probably all they could afford. It didn't cost a lot to feed a big family red beans and rice. We never missed a meal.

We were all over the Houston area. We stayed outside until we were told to come in. During the day we would be in the ditches trying to catch crawdads, then, after the sun went down, we were in the streets trying to catch bats. It was in Houston that I got my first taste of stealing. We mostly stole bikes and other things out of people's yards or garages. We would go to other neighborhoods to do dirt, that way we could move freely back home in our neighborhood. I don't remember the specifics, but I seem to recall running through the wooded areas around the neighborhood when crossing the street, Ballee got hit by a car and died. This was tragic for my Aunt Alma, and I felt that I had lost a friend. I am not callously glossing over this event. His death was my first experience of someone dying. We went from having a great time playing, to not. At Ballee's wake, an adult had to explain to me why Ballee could not get up and play. He looked fine. I'm not going to get psycho-analytical in determining how it affected me. It did. I have repressed memories of Ballee and I want to keep it that way. I refuse to view an open casket of someone I love.

Unkee eventually moved the family to Midland; that's when things went into high gear. It was also around that time that Brad moved to Midland from San Diego. That old saying about "treating someone like a stepchild" —was prevalent in Unkee's household. Wayne and Cuda were Unkee's stepsons, and he treated them like it. He didn't show them much love and they didn't really ask for it.

Let's just say that some of the bad habits that came with them to Midland got on steroids. Yes, I was along for the ride. Our thievery evolved. It went from stealing bikes to stealing cars to breaking into houses and snatching purses. I was there for everything, except the purse snatching. I was never bold enough or fast enough to get into snatching purses like my cousin Cuda, but I was more than willing to help him spend the money. He was more than eager to point out how I didn't put in the work but wanted to enjoy the spoils of war. That was fine with me because it wasn't my thing. Then there was the shoplifting. We were officially banned from K-mart – that was just for the stuff we were caught with. There was this one time that Cuda discovered that the back door of the Toys-R-Us store was open. He went in and cleaned them out. Then we had to go to K-mart and boost some batteries to run all the stuff.

Unkee did not spare the rod. He never laid hands on me, but I witnessed some of the things he did to those boys – his stepkids. As they grew older, the whuppings turned into beatings. It started with belts, then extension cords, then 2 x 4 wooden planks. I even saw him throw a drive shaft at one of them. Unkee had a temper, but I was safe from it either because he feared angering my mom, his older sister, or because he had a genuine disregard toward his stepsons.

My fondest memory of Unkee is when he and I were working in Grannie's den. I was helping him change the clutches out in an automatic transmission. I couldn't have been more than ten. I think it was his first time doing something like this because he was using a Chilton book, which is a mechanic's manual for working on cars. We must have been up till the wee hours of the morning, but we got it finished. I don't know if it worked when he put it back in the car or not. I always assumed it did. I can point to this one moment in time as defining me as being the strong engineer I am today. If I could do that as a kid, nothing machine-related scares me.

Grannie's house was the center of my universe. To this day, I have her address and phone number memorized. 1210 East Cottonwood…682-3815. No matter where I was in the world, I knew I could reach anyone in the family through Grannie, and if anyone needed to get at me, she was where you started. I want to think that we all, at one time or another, lived in Grannie's house. Brad and I spent our best years there. We would get up on the roof and jump off with sheets or garbage bags, and acted like they were parachutes. Grannie had fruit trees that grew pomegranates and peaches. She put the peaches in Mason jars and made preserves out of them. We ate the pomegranates, seeds and all. This was very unpleasant when I realized you can't digest the seeds.

Grannie always cooked a big dinner for everyone to come over and eat. During the Reagan years, she made sure that the lady who lived down the street from her had a meal. This lady lived with a lot of cats, and rumor had it that she ate cat or dog food; it was cheaper than meat. Grannie was always looking out for people. She went to church religiously (pun intended). She kept the family together. Of course, when she died, the family fell apart, but her legacy lives on through us.

I don't think anything I say about my mom – your grandma – will do her justice. She was a single mother raising six kids. As you can tell from the previous stories, I spent a lot of time with others. My mom was busy working two or three jobs. I was the youngest. Brenda and Bobbie were too young to watch me. Junior, Sandra, and Teddy were doing their teen thing, running the streets. I needed adult supervision. This was the reasoning for my staying in Killeen with Aunt Nina or in Houston with Unkee. I believe Grannie was going to school to get some degree. I wish I had talked to her about her going to school.

My mom made it a point to make sure we were not on welfare. Even if it meant that she didn't get to see me that often. As a young child, I don't remember seeing a lot of my mom. I knew she worked at Levi Strauss during the regular work week; as a seamstress making jeans. On the weekend she was cleaning homes for the well-to-do white folks in Midland. Grannie did this as well because teaching didn't really make ends meet, as she would say. Woodrow Beatty, that was his name. Mom would clean his house and he would pay her and give her vanilla sandwich cookies and grapes for us kids. I loved those cookies and grapes. He was married when Mom started cleaning. His wife later died, and he became a widower. He was very old, and Mom worried about him as if he were family. This was and is how she treats people.

    She also cleaned a house for a lady named Agnes, aka Aggie. As I got older and in grade school, sometimes I went with her to help her out. She taught me how to vacuum a floor where you wouldn't leave marks on the carpet that showed you stepped there. These were the tricks of good housekeeping. As I said, she put in work to provide for us. She convinced Aggie to hire me to pull weeds in her yard to earn me some spending money. During the summer Mom had her brother, Unkee, work me around his shop. He didn't have to pay me, but he had to get me school clothes for the upcoming school year. That was usually a bad deal because he would work the hell out of me and not give Mom a dime. She didn't have the extra money to get me clothes, so I would end up with hand-me-downs. She did have to buy me shoes because I would wear mine down until the soles fell off. Going to the Payless shoe store was a treat, even if I ended up with knock-off brand shoes.

Mom smoked a lot, and drank on occasion, especially when she was playing poker at Betty Joe, Ruth, and Jean's house; her friends. I went with her a few times. Most of the time I would be sleeping in the backseat of the car. I don't know what I did to spend the time. I do remember that there was one night when I ate all the grapes that Mr. Beatty had given her. Then I fell asleep and peed all over myself in the backseat. When she woke me up, I started crying because I was wet from head to toe. This memory is burned in my head. Her playing poker wasn't about the gambling. I think it was a de-stressor for her. Sometimes you just need to blow off some steam.

Keep in mind that my mom was 28 when she had me. She was still young, but she had six kids, and that's not a good catch to most men. It goes without saying that none of the men she dated were trying to be "daddy", but I'll say it anyway. I remember one guy, a hustler who talked a good game and ended up taking her money. There was another guy, named Pooch. I think he was a truck driver because he was gone a lot. He only showed up when he wanted something.

As the other kids grew up and moved out, Mom started working for the school district, in the cafeteria. By the time I got to high school, everybody knew my mom. They called her Mrs. Dorn and she hated it because she could not stand Robert. You would think I would have been embarrassed to have my mom as the "cafeteria lady," but I wasn't. First off, she wasn't working at my school. Second, she wasn't cleaning other people's homes anymore. I got to see her more. I loved the fact that she came to my football games. I wanted to make her proud of me because I knew she made an effort.

It broke her heart to hear that I was leaving for the Army after graduation. I know this because she's told me so several times. I've always had her in my corner, even when she wasn't physically there. I never felt abandoned when I was not with her. What I didn't know until later in life was how much she was working in the background trying to get Robert to be a father. She twisted his arm to come to my Basic Training graduation. She twisted his arm to write to me while I was in the Army. I got one letter. She tried to get him to contact me when I was at my lowest. That contact never came, but she was always there. This is one of a thousand reasons I call her every Sunday to this day. She literally saved my life more than twice. This is why I truly believe that without her, there would be no me.

As I write this chapter, I keep coming back to add more stuff. There is so much more to my story, but I know I can't get it all in. Memories are refreshed as I write this, but time is of the essence so I'll have to settle for the main hits. I hope you understand.

Chapter 2
Be All You Can Be

As sad as it is that I'm bad at remembering entire events, some things I'll never forget. I graduated from basic training, and my mom, Robert, and Unkee came to my graduation ceremony. They drove six hours from Midland to El Paso. I was so happy to see them and surprised. I knew my mom was going to be there, but I didn't expect to see my uncle, and I really didn't expect Robert. The thing I remember most was them taking me to the movies. We saw Eddie Murphy's *Coming to America.* I remember Robert going on about how nice the black folks were dressed. I remember them saying that they had to get back on the road. I remember thinking that they had just got there, and I didn't want them to leave. I felt so alone after they left. I remember crying because they left me feeling isolated and without family. I remember that other guys' families stayed for the whole weekend. Why couldn't mine?

I didn't realize that they, my uncle and Mom, had to get back to work. I didn't realize that they probably didn't have the money for a motel to stay any longer. I remember my uncle being proud of me for making it through basic training. It probably wasn't as hard as his, but he knew that it was still tough. I remember my mom keeping me close because she missed "her baby." What I don't remember was Robert telling me that he was proud of me or holding any type of conversation with me about what I went through or how I felt. Just that the black folks were dressed so nice in that movie. This is what I remember.

To this day, I can't think of *Coming to America* without thinking of the pain their visit caused. My heart was broken. I think sometimes what it would have been like had they not shown up. I would hate to put that on my mom because I know she was proud of me and I know she would have stayed as long as I wanted her to. I was so focused on trying to get a reaction out of Robert that I missed everything else. I guess that one bad apple spoiled the bunch.

Basic training was a beast. It was not just the physical demand, but the psychological reconstruction of my character. I use the word "reconstruction" intentionally because the Army demolished what I was and built what was needed to succeed. I went in a boy and came out a soldier.

Those who don't know or who weren't grounded would think this is a good thing. Those who know otherwise, know that this is detrimental to being a person. The Army made me cold and calculating. It probably didn't help my situation having a bad experience with mail call. When you are going through basic training, there's a part of you that realizes the objective of the Army is trying to separate you from your past life, family, and friends in order to make you dependent on Uncle Sam. There is nothing more depressing or demeaning than mail call. You're standing there waiting with the other soldiers, hearing everyone else's name called and seeing their excitement when they get a letter or package. Thinking back, I am truly thankful for the letters I did receive. Those letters and the occasional phone calls were all the contact one had to civilization.

The thing I remember, when it came to letters, was that I received more letters from my best friend, Marc, than I did from Robert – which was ONE. The thing I remember, when it came to phone calls, was that my mom was the one call that I made, and I knew she would be there. I truly believe that is why I call her every Sunday to this day. That's my security blanket. The few letters that I did receive, I held on to them like gold. I read them over and over again. They were my tie to reality. They kept me grounded.

When I was done with basic training, I drowned myself in alcohol. This was pretty much until my nervous breakdown that left me "on my own." This is not the chapter of my life that I wish to focus on now. That's a story for another day. What you need to know was that my personality was developed at this time, and it stuck with me more so than anything else. Good, bad, or indifferent, this was now part of me – the soldier.

The brightest star in my life in the Army was the deal I made when I signed up. They said that they could station me near Bobbie. I went into the Army because she was in the Army, and now I would be able to be near her. I found myself in Neubrücke, Germany – Bravo 4/1 Air Defense Artillery. I was about 12 miles from Baumholder, where Bobbie was stationed. Being with my sister was what mattered. She drove to my base, picking me up in her little Opel, and we went back to Baumholder to hang out because that base was so much bigger, with American restaurants. The Pizza Hut there sold wine with the pizza. Bobbie was into weightlifting, and she had a lot of bodybuilding magazines that she showed me. We spent as much time together as we could. I didn't care about anything that was going on in my company because I was going to hang out with my sister. I cherish those moments. Eventually, she moved on and I was back to being on my own.

Much of my time in the Army is a book in and of itself, but I'm going to focus on the two major occasions. The first was in Germany. Being in Germany was my first time outside of Texas; outside of the United States. It wasn't as much of a culture shock as I thought it would be. First off, the Army gave us a ton of classes on what to do and not to do. This was in 1989-1990, not exactly fresh out of the Cold War, but close enough that we were warned about being approached by individuals looking to recruit U.S. soldiers to be spies. My favorite was the warning of seeing a pack of cigarettes standing up on end in the middle of an outdoor plaza. You were told to ignore it because it might be a bomb. We got a crash course in the German language. We also got a lot of shots; I'm not sure what kind. We didn't ask and they didn't tell.

I don't remember much about the flight there, but I do know that we landed in Frankfurt and were driven to Neubrücke; a two-hour drive. I was finally at my new home, Bravo Company 4/1 Hawk Missile Systems. "If it flies; it dies!" The base was small, and we shared it with the Air Force. This was a point of contention because the Air Force had house cleaners clean their barracks. We were responsible for cleaning our own barracks. In preparation for inspections was the only time we really cleaned. I never could understand the concept of polishing cement until it had a mirror finish. I thought I left all that behind in Basic Training, but that's another story.

On the base was a commissary and a restaurant/bar/club called the Rod & Gun. This was the hang-out spot. Keep in mind that I was still underage by U.S. standards, but here I was fine. Maybe that was the problem, or at least one of the problems. The Army didn't care if you drank alcohol. They didn't really care if you over-indulged. They did care if you missed formation. I learned this early in my Army career in Fort Bliss, Texas, during Advanced Individual Training (A.I.T.). Anyway…the vending machine in our barracks had beer in it. Not good beer, it was Löwenbräu. The taste left something to be desired, but it was available 24 hours a day until the machine was empty.

When it came to beer, being in Germany was the best. For the people who lived off the base and in town, they had a truck that would deliver beer, like the milkman did back in the day in the States. The guy dropped off a full rack of beer at the doorstep and picked up your empty rack. I personally didn't get to experience this because only married soldiers living with their families could stay in town. So, I got my beer from the commissary, the vending machine, or the Rod & Gun. If we had to get beer from the commissary, the rule was, we could only drink what we could carry. I got really good at carrying two cases of beer. This was a problem during the spring and summer because the fridges in the rooms were so small all of the beer couldn't fit, and nobody likes warm beer. During fall and winter, I would stack the beer outside my window on the ledge to keep it cool. Luckily, I was on the second floor. If I went to the Rod & Gun, I got Heineken. They had Heineken in 32-ounce cans. Best beer ever! Of course, I had to have my usual meal; grilled ham and cheese *mit pommes frites* (with french fries).

The commissary was a store on base that sold American-brand everything: groceries, beer, cigarettes, alcohol, laundry detergent, *et cetera*. We were given ration cards for buying hard liquor and cigarettes, but not beer. With the ration card, you were allowed eight cartons of cigarettes and a fifth of hard liquor a month. I didn't smoke or drink hard liquor, so I didn't care. Thinking back, I wonder how the Army felt that it was okay to drink beer like there's no tomorrow, but put limits on bourbon and Marlboros.

The funny thing about American-brand cigarettes is they have a much higher nicotine level than European cigarettes, so they were valuable. The value was so high that my roommate at the time would take cigarettes to Amsterdam and trade them for drugs. I didn't really know all of this until

I came into the room one day, because I had a key, and saw the display on Maxwell's bunk. Little did I know, Maxwell was the drug kingpin for all of Baumholder. I embellish because Maxwell was as bad a drug dealer as Junior. Long story short, when Maxwell realized I didn't smoke, he asked for my rations, which I gave him. I wasn't going to use them. As a "tip" he gave me a choice from his stash. All I'll say is hashish is a hell of a drug and I wasn't the only one in the barracks who felt that way. I believe this is why I don't have clear memories about…well, let's just say…much of my young adulthood. They come and go like screenshots in a PowerPoint presentation.

Every three to six months or so, the company loaded up all the equipment and went to the field to set up the equipment for what can only be described as "war games." in actuality it was a camping trip. We roughed it. We had to eat food that was either cooked in the kitchen and traveled with us or it was cooked in the mess hall on base, packed in containers and brought out to us in the field. During lunch we would eat MREs (Meals Ready to Eat). In the beginning these were the nastiest things I'd ever eaten, but after a while they grew on me. The next thing I knew I was making trades with people to get my favorite – *chicken a la king* with hot sauce. Yes, the MRE came with a tiny bottle of hot sauce. If you wanted the MRE warmed up, you would put it either inside of one of the radars or on the engine of whatever was running.

We worked hard because everything ran off generators and the cables for the equipment, which were about two inches in diameter and were on three-foot spools. We had to connect all the equipment, which were football fields apart from each other. We also played hard because we brought some of our party favors with us, courtesy of Maxwell. So, while in the field, we were required to carry our rifles and be in our combat gear, which included helmets and ammo pouches. We weren't given ammo because this was just an exercise, but you had to carry the magazines for the ammo in the pouches. I would maybe carry two magazines, instead of the required six. In the extra spaces, I carried tools to work on the equipment and a block of hashish. We had a way of making a bong out of an empty coke can. After smoking the hash, we would crush the can and it would look like any other trash.

One time someone forgot to crush their can and the First Sergeant found it. Piss tests were scheduled soon after. The really funny thing was the NCO in charge of the urinalysis was a customer of Maxwell's. We always knew in advance and in a lot of cases our samples either came up missing or got contaminated (watered down). Maxwell was a nefarious adversary for the First Sergeant. The First Sergeant, aka "Top," knew that the small base of Neubrücke was flooded with drugs, but he didn't know where they were coming from. To make matters worse, Maxwell would get high and defecate in the urinals. This drove Top crazy. He would tell the company about how the "shitting bandit" had struck again and that we lost our weekend passes because of it. Long story short, we had a lot of fun, adventure, heartaches, and pains in Bravo 4/1.

As my time wound down in Germany, I was so excited to start my short-timer's calendar. I would mark each day as I got closer to going back to the States. I loved Germany, but it wasn't the same as being home. I had my orders; I was going to be stationed in Fort Hood, Texas. My mind was all over the place thinking about the places where I was going to eat and all the things I was going to do. Then H.W. started a war in Iraq. This caused what the Army calls a stop-loss. I wasn't going home. Yeah, I was bummed out.

I didn't even get to fight because the Iraqi military didn't have an air force, so there was no need for air defense. Patriot battalions were sent to shoot down SCUD missiles because they engaged at further distances than the Hawk missile system. The war lasted 42 days. As soon as the war ended,

I got new orders to leave Germany and go to Fort Hood.

I've said it before and I'll probably say it until I die: If I'm in any part of Texas, I'm home. Being in Fort Hood was like catching a second wind. Unfortunately, I spent a lot of my early time in Fort Hood setting up for a life that never happened, but that's a different story for another time. I suffered from a great depression and I was happy to self-medicate. I moved from hashish and beer to Crown Royal and beer. Shout out to my roomie, Galloway, for introducing me to Crown Royal and the Blues. We would drink Crown Royal by the half-gallon and listen to Otis Redding ("Sitting at the dock of the bay, watching the tide roll away"). We even had a special apparatus that we could put the bottle in and just tip it to pour.

Little did I know, as wild as things got at the 4/1 in Germany, they would pale in comparison with my Fort Hood crew. Some of my early crew from Germany when I first got there were now in Fort Hood, and they put me on real quick. To start things out, I needed to get a car. Let's keep in mind that my credit was crap and my salary in the Army was even worse. Getting a car wasn't easy. I think it was either Bobbie or your grandma who co-signed for me. I wanted to get a GMC Jimmy but couldn't afford it. I ended up getting a two-door Chevy Cavalier. Funny thing is that two other guys in the crew – Big Lew and Charles – had the same car, but different colors.

Having a car in the United States after living in Germany is not a good thing. They drive too slow here. I made it a point to go back to Midland every chance I got. I got a lot of speeding tickets along the way. I even got threatened by a judge in one county to have my license suspended. I went to driver's education classes a lot to get the tickets canceled. This was allowed in those days.

On my trips back to Midland, I was guaranteed to stop at Grannie's and Mom's. I even managed to stop by Robert's house. He was remarried and had a child. He married Trina, whom I knew from when I was growing up and hanging out with Marc and Jason. Jason was a year younger than Marc and I, but always went out with us. Trina was Jason's big sister. I wanted so much to be a part of their family, but things just didn't work out that way. The lasting memory that I do have is that we gathered in prayer when they knew I was heading back to Fort Hood. Robert would ask God to dispatch his angels to ride with me on my journey to ensure my safe return.

When I wasn't driving to Midland, I hung out with the crew. We would have cookouts during the day and hit the clubs at night. We were a rowdy bunch, and we didn't care. Some of the guys just wanted to pick fights. Eventually, we got tired of the club scene in Killeen and started trekking out to Austin. Now believe me when I tell you that I am blessed, and I'll tell you why.

I don't remember too many details. I can't tell you what night it was, but most likely it was a Saturday. I don't remember the season. Hell, I can't even tell you who I was with. I can't tell you the name of the club, but there is a good chance it was on Sixth Street. All I know is that I looked across the floor on the second floor of this club and I saw Marc. Keep in mind that I didn't keep in close contact with Marc while I was in the Army. When he wrote me, during basic training, I would always write back. While I was in Germany, I don't think we stayed in touch. When I got to Fort Hood, I know we didn't contact each other. While I went away to the Army, Marc went away to Texas A&M. I hadn't seen him since high school graduation. If I hadn't said it before, I'll say it now, Marc is my best friend (period). Long story short, we picked up where we left off. This began my transitional idea of getting out of the Army.

After finding Marc, I spent a lot of weekends in Austin. We would hit Sixth Street, play dominoes, and shoot dice. Man, it was good to be back with my boy. Spending time with him kept me sane, but it also put me in the mood of realizing that I was done with the Army. I remember the weekend before I was to get out, my ETS

(Expiration of Term of Service) day, we were up until the early morning, and I still had to drive two and a half hours to get back to the base. I was tired and still drunk, and I fell asleep at the wheel. I woke up because my car hit a mile marker sign or something on the side of the road and it shattered my passenger side windows, sending glass into my face. That, and the cold air, sobered me up. I made it back to base and got my clearing papers. It was time to start my new chapter.

My first stop was home: Midland, Texas. I ended up staying with Grannie after getting out of the Army, but it didn't last long. I didn't really have a plan as to what I was going to do as a civilian. For whatever reason, maybe because I didn't have a job and was just hanging around the house, but I somehow got pulled into having to go to the Freshman High School to talk to the principal about my nephew. She had been my Spanish teacher when I was in school. Anyway, she insisted that I take responsibility for handling my nephew's issues. I wasn't ready for that. I called Marc that night and asked if he needed a roommate.

I'd barely lasted a month in Midland before I had my bags packed, heading to Austin. Marc only had a one-bedroom apartment, and he was under a lease, but he let me sleep on the couch, at a discounted rate. Yeah, he still wanted me to pay rent. I told you that he didn't play when it came to finances. For the next three months, I collected unemployment checks and didn't even attempt to look for a job. I figured that I needed a vacation after seven-plus years in the Army.

Marc and I had this pastime of playing NCAA football on Sega Genesis. We would take the worst team, usually Washington State, and go through whole seasons to win the championship. During my "vacation." I was usually sitting on the couch playing video games when he came home from work. I'd pass him a beer, a Keystone Light, and we'd get the season started. Eventually, I realized that I needed to get to work, literally. So, I took a job at a temp agency that landed me at an electronics company called Atlas (to become Arrow). I would get paid $7.50 an hour scraping the labels off semiconductors. After his lease was up, we moved into a two-bedroom apartment, and I moved the rest of my stuff from Midland. We played a lot of NCAA football and drank a lot of beer. So much so that one morning, Marc had to take me to the hospital for alcohol poisoning.

We went out almost every weekend. I remember that we were at a party, and I was talking to a lady. She was talking about getting her MBA. She asked me if I knew what that was. I didn't. I felt so stupid. I started attending classes at the Austin Community College. My goal was to get enough credits to transfer to the University of Texas.

Between having my heart broken, the self-medication, and the drama, I managed to develop a love for behavioral science; psychology, to be specific. This was why I worked to get into the University of Texas. While I was still in the Army, I would read *Psychology Today* magazines, thinking this was for me. I realized that one of the bi-products of being a soldier was the dumbing-down. I had a hard time spelling. It was an eye-opening moment. I got what I needed out of the Army, a G.I. Bill for college, and the life skills of a soldier.

Chapter 3
On My Own

The hardest thing that I ever had to do was try to get out of the Army. The actual act of getting out wasn't the problem. I had already met the minimum requirement, which was staying in four years, because of the job I was trained for as a Missile Systems Technician. The hard part was trying to break the dependency. In the Army, I knew my job, I knew where to sleep and eat, I knew where to go if I got sick, and most importantly, I knew that the check was coming at the end of the month. I had no idea what I would do as a civilian.

It's funny that I would call this chapter "On My Own." You would think that I've been on my own since leaving for the Army, but that's not the whole truth. Even in the Army, I didn't feel alone. I was a part of a team, which I would call "family." I truly believe that this chapter in my life (pun intended) prepared me to be the person that I am today. I'm much stronger now because I had to rebuild my life. I like to reference "Humpty

Dumpty" because it exemplified my life at this time. I had a bad fall from what must have been a very high wall and I didn't have the king's men to put me back together again. What I did have was a phenomenal therapist who showed me that I possessed the strength and ability to put myself together . . . but I'm jumping too far ahead.

My story started a little before I got out of the Army. Three consecutive catastrophes happened in a year, and it was too much for me to handle. I cannot recall which came first, and I'm not even sure what year it was in, because that was another life, a lifetime ago. The culmination of these events made me want to take my own life.

In no particular order, because I cannot give you one, the first event was the rejection of my first love. I've only loved two women in my life, outside of the family. I was going to spend the rest of my life with her. We met in Germany while we were both in the Army. It might have been a point of opportunity; it might have been the fact that she was the first white woman that I had been with, and our time together was the longest relationship I had ever been in. Whatever the case, this was what I knew about love.

I came back to the U.S. first and we would communicate by mail; snail mail because there was no such thing as email. The waiting was excruciating. I'm sure a psychosis developed during this time. Long story short, I asked her to marry me; she said "Yes." Some time went by and then a letter eventually came that said otherwise. My heart was smashed. The lesson from this is don't get between a woman and her family. If the family doesn't want you, it's not going to end well.

My second devastation came when my Aunt Nina died. She was a Danish white lady in a family of blacks and I'm sure she felt some kind of isolation. But I felt nothing but love for her because that's what I felt coming from her. She was always there to comfort me when my mom wasn't. As I stated before, she was a classy lady.

She eventually moved to Houston, I think, while I was in the Army. She wrote me more times than Robert did. I recall being a self-absorbed ass and not giving her the time of day. I recall driving all over the state of Texas in my two-door Chevy Cavalier and not going to visit her ONCE. I recall her dying. Rumor had it that she took her own life because she was lonely. I was devastated because all I had to do was be there for her like she was for me. What an ass I was. She didn't deserve that.

The third event that tipped me over the edge was while I was working an internship for the Texas State Hospital in the Juvenile ward. I was out of the Army and attending UT to get my degree in Psychology. I remember thinking that working at the State Hospital would be so nice for my résumé.

I didn't realize what I was in for. A young gentleman was brought to the ward for evaluation because he had been arrested and he told the authorities that he wanted to hurt himself. They put them up for evaluation. I guess the doctor(s) thought he was just saying it to avoid jail. He was not put on suicide watch or anything. At least, on suicide watch, the person is placed in the hallway where they can be observed. Long story short, we found him the next morning hanging from the ceiling. His name was Christopher. I was in shock. I didn't see it coming. No one's life is worth taking to avoid the consequences of his own actions. I wasn't ready for this. I and the other staff at that ward were fired that morning for failure to properly monitor the patient, even though he was not on suicide watch. That was fine with me because I don't think that I was strong enough to stay on the job. I took the job, especially in the Juvenile section, because I was heavily into Child Development. I wanted to get the kids off to a good start. I'd bitten off more than I could chew.

    I went to Austin to get my old job back, but there were no openings. They did have an opening in Phoenix if I wanted it. I wanted it. I needed to get away from this. I needed to get back to the predictability of machines. I needed a reality break. I moved to Phoenix. I left everything. I dropped out of college as a senior, so close to graduating. I got to Phoenix and buried myself in work and alcohol. I tried to leave my emotions behind; buried.

> [Side Note – while writing this: you, my son, are so much as I was when I was young; so emotional. I hope you read this and avoid the pitfalls that I experienced when it comes to dealing with your emotions. I guess I better get this written before you get too old.]

I worked the night shift in Phoenix, which was literally cool with me because I don't think that I could have afforded the utility bills trying to keep the apartment cool during the summer. You know it's hot when it is still 98° at 11:30 at night. I recall driving on the highway at 90+ mph and then accelerating into the turn hoping that the car would flip. No, I wasn't wearing a seat belt. I would drive while extremely drunk. I was wild and loose. I wanted to die, but I wanted it to be natural. I wanted to take my own life, but I needed it to be something that "just happened." I was playing Russian Roulette with my car. I didn't feel or see the need to keep living. I didn't see the value in my life. I didn't see suicide as wrong. Aunt Nina did it. Christopher did it.

I guess all of those prayers that my mom and Grannie gave kept my car from flipping, but I kept my emotions buried. The one thing that people should understand is that you may think that you have control of your emotions, and you may think that you can live a life without being emotional or showing emotion, but when your emotions want to get your attention, there's nothing you can do to stop it.

So, there I was one night, sitting at a traffic light, waiting for it to change. I had just left the Glendale Community College campus after attending some class for something. I can't tell you what was playing on the stereo or what I was thinking at the time. All I know was that I sat at that light for a really long time. It wasn't because the light wasn't working; it had changed several times. It wasn't like I couldn't move, paralyzed by emotion. I just didn't move. When I finally realized that I wasn't moving, that's when I realized I was crying. My emotions wanted out, so they got my attention. I had taken enough psychology classes to realize that this wasn't normal. I knew I needed help.

The insurance plan through the company I worked for was great back in those days. I found a psychiatrist who was on the insurance plan, and I took that first step to get help. I can't bad-mouth the psychiatrist because she diagnosed me as bipolar and drugged me up hard. It helped to take the edge off, but it didn't identify or resolve my issues. The medication she put me on (Lithium, Wellbutrin, and a few others to regulate my heart rate) made me feel like the walking dead. I had no emotional response to anything. I didn't have highs or lows. I was on cruise control, just making it through the day. Half the time, I didn't even know what day it was. I don't remember her telling me not to drink alcohol while on the medication, or I didn't hear her.

It took a psychologist to help me. He knew that psycho-pharmaceuticals were not going to fix my problems. They were just going to put me in a state of not caring about anything. He talked with me and asked a lot of questions. He was a therapist. He wanted to discover what my problem was so we could fix it. I had lost my identity. Truth is, I never really established an identity for myself. I was just bits and pieces that made up me. I was fractured and unstable.

One of the issues I had identifying who I was had to do with Robert. During this time of discovery, I reached out to my mother, and she knew that I couldn't come to grips with who I was. She reached out to Robert so that he would contact me; to rescue me. His help never came. That's when I realized that I would have to figure this out, not on my own, but without him.

My therapist rocked and it didn't hurt that he was a black man. He gave me a book to read: *King,*

Warrior, Magician, Lover: Rediscovering the Archetypes of the Mature Masculine, by Robert Moore and Doug Gillette. This book literally changed my life. After reading the book, I realized that my strengths are the archetypes of a magician and a warrior. Magician because I can make machines work. I was a great technician, an outstanding PC dude (I built PCs for other people for beer), and a decent engineer. Warrior, because I was a soldier, and soldiers fight.

I fought back to gain control of my life and to get off the medication that made me feel like a zombie. I fought to identify myself. I called it egocentricity because it was all about me. Like a rubber band that snaps back, I went to an extreme to identify me, and there were some casualties along the way. I guess that's the price of war, but that's another story. This was the mentality of me back then. Long story short, I moved to Reno, Nevada, where I met my future wife and her three kids.

This was only possible because of what I had gone through. I was now ready to move to the next chapter in my life. I knew who I was and, with that, I was prepared to evolve. It wasn't until your birth, Liam, that I truly gave value and identification of what it meant to be a Dorn. Everything that Robert wasn't for me, I would be for you. We would make this name ours. We are

Dorn and we will conquer the world. This was my mentality from your conception. I was no longer on my own.

Chapter 4
Stepping Up to Bat

Before there was you, Liam, there were your brothers and sister. To make a long story short, I met Karima at the company that transferred me from Austin to Phoenix and then to Reno. We were coworkers until she went on to work for another company. We kept common friends and eventually went out on a date or two. There was something about the way she carried herself and the boots she wore. There is no way I could talk about her and not mention the boots. The boots came up to cover her calves and were made of the finest leather. The fit was like a glove and the way she walked was hypnotic or should I say hip-notic. Anyway, as we dated, we became friends. I wanted to be there for her, to help her in any way I could.

Rent was getting high for both of us and I couldn't see why we needed to have two separate apartments, so I moved in with her. The funny thing is that her having three kids never was a determining factor. I knew I was going to marry her right after I moved into the apartment with them. That's when I discovered my princess. She, of all of Karima's kids, showed me love first. She hugged me for the first time at bedtime and I knew from that moment that I would do anything to keep her safe.

I now had a family to take care of and I dropped my walls for them. They helped me define me. I was now "Mike," not stepdad or dad, but "Mike." I know that's my name, but they would say it with respect and love; and I would do anything to earn that respect and love. This was (and still is) my family. I was not hung up on the fact that they weren't my kids biologically.

Farhad was the man of the house. I was more than happy to relieve him of that responsibility. He did a great job, but he needed to develop into his own man. I do believe that we were friends before I even moved in with them. He would download Dragonball Z stuff and have his mom give it to me.

Ali was (and still is) the strongest kid I've ever known. Not many adults could deal with the physical crap he had to deal with and not break. This child had to have blood transfusions (infusions) every three weeks and then get his stomach poked with a needle every night for his medication to be administered through a pump, while he slept. After Karima and I married, I wanted to be the one to take him to the hospital. I wanted to normalize this part of his life as much as I could. I wanted this to be our time to eat out. I wanted this to be our bonding time. It was hard sometimes watching inexperienced nurses trying to put an I.V. on him. He would be in so much pain and start crying, but they had to keep trying until they got it, no matter how many times they poked him. His strength in dealing with his thalassemia was the blueprint that I would find myself following.

Heala, my princess was (and still is) my shining light, my dawn. As I have stated, she was the first one to show me love. She was the first one to make me feel welcome. We never really set aside "bonding time," as I did with Ali, but we bonded, nonetheless.

Karima, my queen, is the strongest woman I've ever met, second to my mother. She never needed me. She wanted me and that attracted me to her. She possessed the values of both of my mothers. The sheer strength of my mom and the class of my Aunt Nina.

I love the fact that we have dinner at the dining table as a family, and we talk. We laugh too. Back in the day, before you, Liam, were born, our favorite dinner conversation was based on *The Simpsons*. Karima doesn't watch the show, but the kids and I love it. The fun part about our dinner ordeal started with someone either saying a random quote or reference about the topic at that time, with a Simpsons' quote. Ninety-eight percent of the time, it was a quote from *The Simpsons,* and then we recalled a variety of scenes from that particular episode. We laughed a lot.

We always had an open-concept house, literally and metaphorically, even before I knew what that was. We sat around and just hung out, talking about anything. I don't remember too much about the apartment when I moved in with them. I do remember our first house. It was kind of tight, but Farhad moved out and that gave Heala and Ali their first experience of having their own rooms. Now keep in mind that, when Karima and I got married, we were barely making ends meet. The struggle was real. Our first house was the best we could afford at the time, especially since rent prices were getting outrageous. We had a roof over our heads, clothes on our backs, and food to eat. We had everything we needed and some of what we wanted. My main mission was, and still is, to make sure that this is always the case. I grew up on the other side of that coin and I don't want my kids to experience that, but I digress; that's another story.

The neighborhood of our first house was new. Heala and Ali made friends and they were always busy playing with them. I wired the house with ethernet connections so we could connect Xboxes in multiple rooms. Then the kids, their friends, and I played Halo and fought in groups, in different rooms around the house. That was so much fun.

I remember the first time I had to pick up the kids from school. I remember the anxiety I had thinking I wouldn't be able to pick them out of the sea of kids coming out of the classes, but I spotted them. I think that was the time I realized that I didn't really focus on their faces, like I would do with a stranger I had just met. I figured I wouldn't need to since we lived in the same house. That eventually changed to where I would never let them out of my sight. The first phase of the "helicopter parent."

We were married and all was right with the world. I was fine with raising my stepkids, but Karima wanted a baby. This frightened me – terrified me. One particular song came to mind, Anthony Hamilton's "Comin' Where I'm From – Too scared to have kids…and do like daddy did… cuz I'm so scared of failin'…"[8] I didn't want to be like the father that I had had. I thought to myself, "I don't want this kid growing up not knowing who I am. I don't want this kid being messed up like me." Once her mind was set on having a baby, I couldn't stop her. This is what I love about her. I'm glad I couldn't stop her because what happened afterward changed the whole game.

On June 29, 2005, I learned of your conception. I started writing in this golden notebook that I had been carrying around. I want to share with you those entries.

7/6/2005: This was your first ultrasound and I saw your heart beat. Your mom has been carrying you for about 8 weeks. The ultrasound has you measured at about 1 cm, about the size of a pea, with a heart rate of 158 bpm. My mom (your grandmother) and your mom's OBGYN said that you are very healthy. Your delivery date is scheduled for February 17-20, 2006.

8/3/2005: Today I saw you take shape. Your mom got your second ultrasound and right away I noticed your head. It looks like you got a lot of knowledge, like your dad. I also saw your hand. It was a beautiful thing to see your five little fingers. Your mom told me that you were moving around a lot. I hate that I missed it, but in order to make the big bucks (sarcasm) I had to travel out of the country for work. I don't plan on letting that happen again.

8/5/2005: Last night you gave me and your mother a big scare. We thought we were going to lose you. I realized for the first time in my life that there was something in this world that I wasn't prepared to let go of. Luckily, we went to the doctor's office and we could see that you were doing fine. Don't scare us like that; I'm too old for that kind of stress.

8/24/2005: Today we found out you are a boy. As your mom always said, it wasn't important if you were a boy or a girl, just as long as you were healthy. Your sister (Heala) wanted a girl and your brother (Ali) wanted a boy. I'm sure Heala will take care of you and love you just as much. We've already started working on your name. Your mom has already banned the use of my name. She says that one "Michael" is enough. That's fine by me because I want you to be unique in your own right, like me. You will have my family name "Dorn." It's not a family name filled with tradition. The name "Dorn" is what we (you and I) make it. But anyway, the front-runner for your name is "Liam Mitchell Dorn," "Mitch" to your friends. When you grow a little more in the womb, I'll have you kick your mom if you like it, to help us get ready for your birth.

8/29/2005: I told your grandmother about your name today and she loved it. She's going to pass it around for reactions. I can't give you a name without appeal.

9/29/2005: Wow! It's been a whole month since I last "talked" to you. I don't want you to think I forgot about you because I didn't. I can't forget about you. There isn't a day that goes by that I don't think about you. Right now, you're about

20 weeks from conception. You're quite active kicking your mom. She says you kick when you like what she's eating, but she also says you kick when you don't. We're still trying to figure that one out. I don't really care for the reason, just as long as you're kicking. I hope it's because you're happy. I have a picture of your face (from the last visit with the doctor). You look just like your old man.

12/8/05: Man! It's been a long time since I've written in this. I just noticed that I began the last entry like that. I didn't write that I haven't "talked" to you this time because I've been talking to you as you jump around in your mom's belly. You are in your 30th week, so your ears are developed. I know you can hear me. I don't really have any breaking news to report. I just wanted to share my thoughts with you. It's been and is still being, a wild ride preparing for your arrival. We are in the homestretch. There are so many variables concerning your arrival. With each variable comes a different issue that starts your mom and me to question ourselves on whether or not we are being good parents in our decisions. The first is whether or not to breastfeed you. Your mom did it with the other kids but complained about them being crybabies. I've read a lot of opinions from "experts" and they all say that breastfeeding is best for the development of the child. We're deciding to go with formula though. It's not that we don't want the best for you, but it's the decision that your mom feels is best for you. The biggest issue is daycare. Even your doctor put in her 2¢, saying that you should not go to a daycare center until you are at least two years old. That's going to be hard with both your mom and me needing to work. Rishi, a friend of mine, suggested that we send you to stay with your grandmother. I'm sure that would be good for you, but I can't consider that an option. You are my only son, my flesh and blood, and it would kill me inside not to see you every day. So we are trying to find other options. I guess you can say that listening to everyone's opinions is working my nerves. I wish we could keep you home until you're old enough for school, but that's not how it's going to be.

1/9/06: Happy New Year! Today you are 34 weeks and 1 day old, after conception. We went in today to have an ultrasound done. The doctor (Hernandez) was worried about your growth. This, of course, made us worry. But everything came out okay. They measured your head, abdomen, and thigh bone (femur). The doctor says that your growth is right on target and that you weigh about 5 pounds. It was cool to have the ultrasound because it's better to be safe than sorry and it was good to see you. We got some good pictures out of it. The camera loves you, boy. We got a great profile of your face and I think you have my nose. We also got a shot of your "business" and all I can say is, "That's my boy!"

From Karima's first ultrasound, all I could see was a speck, but that was life; that was my child and I was hooked. This single moment of life solidified my identity. All of those years of growing up a Dorn amongst the Mills and Scurlocks, I was lost and searching. At this first sign of life, all of that washed away. We are Dorn. We are going to put this name on the map. I don't need Robert to validate me having his last name. The name is now mine and I proudly give it to my child and be there every day of my life so that he knows, without a shadow of a doubt, that his dad loves him.

When the second ultrasound showed us the sex I said, "That's my boy!" My quest was complete. I had a chance to do with you all that I had desired so much from Robert. The third ultrasound was in 3D, and it was a perfect shot of your face. I remember bragging to Karima that you had my nose. Little did I know that you would end up a mini-me.

The hardest part of being an expectant parent is waiting and worrying. The doctors didn't help with all their tests and questions. Because of Karima's and my ages, we were told about the chances of you having Down Syndrome. I also had to take a blood test to see if I carried sickle cell traits. We were warned that if I did, and your mom being a thalassemia carrier, that it would be in our best interest to terminate the pregnancy. Needless to say, this was the last test we would be taking. This was way too stressful for hypotheticals. We vowed that we were going to finish the pregnancy and love you, no matter what.

Realizing that we were moving forward, we went to work on the name. Thanks (sarcasm) to George Foreman for naming all his sons after himself, this option was taken off the table. In the end, that was fine by me. I wanted my son to blaze trails that I couldn't even fathom. I wanted your name to have purpose, power, and meaning. I know I've told you this a few times. We decided to name you "Liam" because it means protector (Irish). The closest I could get to "Michael" that would fit was "Mitchell", which is a derivative of "Michael" meaning "Who is like God?" The last name was a given; Dorn (German) meaning thorn. You have a name, and it was methodically selected just for you. Together we are Dorn.

> [Side Note 12/04/17] I do believe in love at first sight. I have loved you since your conception. Before I knew if you were a boy or a girl, I loved you. Your mom mended my broken and confused heart, but I was still

cynical. Your existence removed that cynicism and filled my heart with love. Now it overflows and life is better.

My family is my life. I am made better; I have purpose. I am driven; because of my family. This is what my queen has given me. I wouldn't have thought that this would have been my life. I just followed one bright path to the next. The signs presented themselves and I was smart to take advantage of them. I hit a home run. Get it? Stepping up to bat and hitting a home run. You can't hit the ball if you don't step up and swing.

You were born on February 18, 2006, at 2:13 a.m., and the rest is history.

Chapter 5
My Family

So much of my childhood through my young adulthood stemmed from identity: belonging; family. I now have a family that is mine. We are not a conventional family. Other than you and me, you wouldn't be able to tell that we are all related because we don't "favor" (as Grannie would say) one another. The key is to watch us interact with each other, then you would know. This is because what we have is love.

From this, we grew, and continue to grow. I married Karima and that automatically got me three kids. I couldn't wait for my family to meet her. I knew that she would be welcomed with open arms, and she was. I was a little worried about meeting her side of the family. I'd wonder if they would have issues with her marrying a black man. I wondered if they would have issues with her marrying an *American* who is a black man.

I believe her nephew, Walid, was the first of her blood relatives that I met. It was awkward because I did not speak Farsi and I couldn't get in the middle of their conversations. I enjoyed the fact that your mom had family, aside from the kids, that she could be herself with. This was important to me because this is the freedom I feel when I'm around my family in Texas. I get to be black. When she is *free*, she gets to be Afghan. When I say "free" I speak of "letting one's hair down." This speaks to the nature of being yourself. We wear different masks and have different personalities with each mask to fit in the environment we are in. This is the way we navigate through our lives in America. I like it when Karima is free to be who she's always been.

I remember the first time her niece Maryam came from Canada to visit. I felt like I was being graded. It's amazing how much my southern, Texan, black culture and upbringing match with that of Afghan culture. Maryam fit right in and we got along great. When we first met, it was with a handshake. When she left to go back to Canada, it was with a hug. That's how we (Texans & Afghans) treat family. It warms my heart to remember that when she came to visit a second time, for Christmas, it started off with a hug.

Then there was Ehsan and Sadaf, Karima's niece and her husband from Afghanistan. They stayed with us while they got situated with getting relocated into the United States. Ehsan was an interpreter for U.S. companies in Afghanistan, which made him a target for the Taliban. That's why the U.S. government had a special visa program to get them out of the country. I remember having a discussion with Karima about the fact that Ehsan had a cousin in Sacramento, and me asking as to why they didn't stay with them. She asked, "What about me?" She missed having family around. I got it. There was nothing more to discuss.

It was tough watching those two get started. The money was tight, and they had to go on welfare. Keep in mind that this was better than living in Afghanistan, but it brought back bad memories of my childhood and the struggle. It brought to light why Grannie had Sunday dinner at her house all the time. That Sunday dinner was probably the best meal we would have for the week. I don't know if that was the struggle that Sadaf and Ehsan had, but after they moved out to their own apartment, I was relieved and looking forward to having them over for dinner. It made me feel useful. It gave me purpose. I wanted to look out for them because they were and still are family.

From a high to a low, we found out that Sadaf was pregnant with their first child. I couldn't wait to spoil this kid. Then we found out that they were moving to Washington state, near Seattle, an over-10-hour drive away. I was saddened by the news. I think that they would have been better off staying close to us, in case they needed anything. I get why they were moving. Ehsan had two cousins and their families around to hang out with, which is what he didn't have in Reno. I interviewed Ehsan about living in America and the differences with Afghanistan for a class. I asked what he missed most about Afghanistan. He told me that we are too isolated in the United States and that when we are done at work, we go our separate ways. No one hangs out to talk and drink tea. He's right. We work, no play, then we go home to work some more, and then rest for the next day. This is the sad reality of our lives. So, I got why they were moving. It would be a better quality of life, in the long run, for them.

Last, definitely not least, is the oldest one's new family. Farhad got engaged to Ashley and Ashley has a daughter from her first marriage, named Presley. Presley is our first grandchild, and she is a blast. I was going to call her "my princess," but that's Heala's title, so she is "my angel."

Farhad and Ashely asked Karima and me what we would want to be called by Presley. I told them that I was perfectly fine with being "Mike." Then I had time to think about it. I decided that I would like to be "Grandpa Mike." I feel that I earned this, and I want to be that part of their life. We are family.

This part of the story, you, Liam, are aware of, so there's nothing you don't know, but it gives context to what drives me and gives me purpose – my family.

Chapter 6
After Diagnosis (My M.S.-Multiple Sclerosis)

While I was washing dishes, around 8:00 p.m. on July 17, 2012, I got a sharp pain on the left side of my head. On a scale of 1 to 10, it was a 9. It almost brought me to my knees. The sharp pain lasted more than 10 seconds; less than 30 seconds. It was like an ice pick stabbing my head. I had a general headache the rest of the night, with the sharp pain returning a few more times, but only lasting for a few seconds. I woke up feeling like I was on lithium again. *Zombie!* My eyes were sensitive to light. I don't remember how I got to work. I don't remember what I did at work. I hate feeling like this. I tried to get in to see the doctor but could only get an appointment for Thursday. It was Wednesday. On the next day, Thursday, the whole day felt like I was drunk. It took a lot of energy to focus on one thing. This is not normal. The doctor's exam did not show anything except that he didn't find a reflex in my right leg. My blood pressure was normal. I declined the offer to take anti-anxiety medication. I requested an MRI. I was told that it would take seven days for pre-approval. The following day, Friday, I woke up feeling hungover. At 9:07 a.m., the "lights" came on and everything was back to normal. Based on some of the engineering change orders that I had submitted that were incomplete, and missing a lot of information, I must have been cruising through my day. After my senses came back, it became eerily obvious that I had no memory of the previous day after the sharp pain incident.

On July 25, 2012, I got an MRI. On July 27th, I was told about the lesions. Worst day ever! The report read "Numerous supratentorial white matter lesions with lesion-morphology and distribution consistent with advanced multiple sclerosis (M.S.)."

How could this be? Bobbie has M.S., not me. This wasn't right. Something was wrong, but there it was, in black and white. From the parking lot of the doctor's office, I called my mother to tell her what they found. Then I cried.

For the next year and some months, I saw a neurologist, and a lot of tests were done. He wasn't completely sold on the fact that I had M.S., and neither was I. I had to have circulation tests where they had sensors on my arms and legs to track blood as it circulated through my body. I had an EKG. I even had to drive to San Francisco to see a specialist at the UCSF Neurology Department. The tests that I had to do there were different from the ones my neurologist did, but they told the story. The UCSF doctor was surprised that I wasn't on medication. The last bit of hope that I'd been misdiagnosed began to leave my consciousness. After returning to Reno, I had to have a spinal tap. Up to this point, I only recalled that Spinal Tap was a movie about some rock band. It was weird how they had me lying face down on this X-ray machine and the doctor looking at my spinal cord as he looked for a place to stick me with the needle. Now, after this procedure, they tell you to lie down until the area can heal, but you were taking swimming classes and I needed to take you. I had to sit in the uncomfortable plastic chairs for an hour; I paid for it later. Who would have thought getting a needle poke in the spine would be so painful?

  I didn't want to believe what was happening, so I stayed in denial. December 5, 2012, was the last entry in my journal. I was keeping it to keep tabs of my symptoms and overall condition. I stopped. I was convinced that I didn't need to keep a journal because I didn't have M.S. My doctor never actually said that I had M.S. He never said I didn't, either. That changed on December 20, 2013.

He verbally and formally confirmed that I have M.S. New worst day ever! I called my mom and told her what the neurologist said, then I cried.

I had my five-day pity-party with only one guest, me. Then it was Christmas Day. I needed to be the father and make sure my family had a good Christmas. I needed to leave the sadness at the door. I didn't spend that time dwelling on "why me?" I guess I didn't think that knowing why would matter too much. I focused more on *What do I do now?* I needed a plan. I didn't like not having control of my future. It was bad enough that I didn't know what the next year was going to look like, but, little did I know, I couldn't even anticipate what the next day was going to be like. The unpredictability of this disease is probably the worst symptom to deal with.

All I could focus on was being there for you to grow up with. I wanted you to have your dad around. I asked God for ten years. I figured you would be 16 and well on your way to being the man I had molded and modeled for you to be. This was my ten-year goal. Later, I realized what I had asked for.

> [Side Note 10/28/15] I know I wasn't specific about how I wanted the 10 years to be, and I am thankful that I could bring you (Liam) to the Coconut Bowl for your soccer team

celebration. I just wish I could have done more. I've hamstrung myself. I'm taking this class; I need to watch my drinking. I can't drink with the rest of the parents. And then I have this M.S. on me so I can't bowl, walk around, or even stand too long. I asked for 10 years, and I still want the 10, but this sucks.

[Side Note 01/03/16] I refer to it as "the" M.S. or "this" M.S., but it's *my* M.S. No two people have the same. Mine acts differently than those of others. Good, bad, or indifferent, it's mine for the rest of my life. My M.S. and me…

I'd give it back if I could, but who'd want it? No, it's stuck with me like glue. I wonder if this would qualify for the Acceptance and Commitment Therapy (ACT) that we briefly talked about in a Psychology class. Maybe I'll look into that one of these days. I get accepting my M.S., because what else can I do? I cannot live in denial, that's just dangerous. I cannot ignore the signs. I cannot just not have a treatment plan. I cannot just leave it in God's hands. *I love you Grannie, but that's just not me.* I must accept it. I'm falling short on committing. I'm too focused on getting through each day. That's my mission. My goal is to finish the day, to get started with the next. I'll figure the rest out after I get my 10 years.

Much of my life centers on being a "soldier." This was not how I was raised, but this is what stuck. The definition I like is "a skilled warrior." There is always a battle. I fight to be a better father than the one I had. This sometimes causes me to fight myself. My depression can get me down, but it cannot keep me there. I have work to do. This battle is daily, hourly, and in some cases, by the minute.

> [Side Note 04/03/16] To be unable to do things men do is dehumanizing. "When you're a man, action is what's expected."[3] (Talib Kweli – *Push Through.*) M.S. is not just taking away my mobility; it's taking away my manhood.

The worst part about my M.S. is that it attacks slowly and indirectly. It had been attacking me for years before D-Day (Diagnosis Day) and I just wrote it off as something else. One example would be getting dressed for work in the morning. I could get dressed standing up and I didn't have to worry about which leg goes first or falling over. I could just put on my pants (still one leg at a time) and my socks just by bending over and getting it done.

Then I began to lose my balance, so I had to lean against the wall in the closet. It's a good thing we have a good-sized walk-in closet. Then it progressed to having to place my pants on the floor and start by putting the right leg in first. I don't know which is worse, trying to balance on the bad leg (right leg) or trying to lift the bad leg to get it in the pants while balancing on the good leg. I can still balance a little on the good leg. Some days I forget to put the bad leg first, then frustration sets in. Stop. Breathe. I tell myself, "Let's not start the day this way because we got a lot more to do."

Then one day a chair showed up in the closet. I guess we had extra folding chairs and your mom felt it would be more useful for me here. I was mad for all of two seconds and then I sat down and put on my socks. I wonder if it's because she heard me stumbling about trying to get dressed or was it because it took me ten minutes – it felt like twenty.

At this time of writing, I'm still at the point of standing to put on my pants, bad leg first. I sit to put on my socks and shoes. I must physically grab my bad leg and put it across the good one to get my sock on and then manually put the foot in the shoe, then stand up to get the shoe on. By the way, by the end of some days, I need that seat to even take off my shirt.

The point of my story is that all of this has

happened over a period of years. I didn't just wake up to this. It was slow and incremental. I wrote it off as one thing or another, but the whole time, it was my M.S. rearing its ugly head. I just came up with another song; Roberta Flack's "Killing Me Softly." "Strumming my pain with his (my M.S.'s) fingers; Singing my life with his words; Killing me softly with his song."[4] (Music is a conduit.) My M.S. attacked slowly and indirectly.

> [Side Note 01/08/18] While reading my Emotional Intelligence 2.0, I've been put into a position to examine my feelings. I tried to avoid this. I sat and asked myself, "How do you feel?" I feel alone and isolated. After D-Day, I looked for sympathy, support, understanding, anything. It wasn't there. This is why I held my own pity party and no one else was invited. My M.S. isn't the same as anyone else's, so we can only share so much of the experience. In a way, I isolated myself and now I'm dealing with the outcome – loneliness.

A family friend who was aware of my M.S. told me about a friend of his who went from being in a wheelchair to walking. He was under the impression that she had M.S. – or maybe I just assumed that she did, and this was why he brought it to my attention. In any case, he wanted me to meet her. I was excited because if it were true, then maybe I could learn her secret. I wanted to witness this miracle. But she didn't have M.S. She had a different disease – Traverse Myelitis. They are similar in nature, as it is an attack on the central nervous system, but it's not the same. That bummed me out.

Little did I know that this visit had planted a seed. As we were leaving the Starbucks, Nicole handed me one of her side-sticks (forearm crutches) to try out. It was not adjusted to my height, and I didn't really feel comfortable holding it. From there on, I connected with her on Facebook and followed her on her many adventures. I thought to myself, "This is a strong person who's picked herself up and stops at nothing." She was and still is an inspiration.

[Side Note 03/25/18] I refer to Nicole as my shepherd, not in the noun sense of the word, but the verb. As a verb, it is defined as: to guide or guard in the manner of a shepherd. Nicole guided me into accepting my disability with pride and to not be ashamed of who I was, a man with a disability. In the beginning, I referred to her as Darth Vader, trying to get me to come to the "dark side." It was the total opposite.

She was leading me to the light. After coming to grips with the fact that my mobility was here to stay and getting worse, I had to get past my pride in accepting the fact that I had a disability and that this is life for me.

Sometime after meeting Nicole, I remember putting my cane in my truck. This is the cane I bought for our trip to Disneyland. That cane sat in the truck for 2 weeks before I finally decided to use it at work. The point was, I needed it because my mobility had gotten so bad that I had to grab Rishi's arm one day to keep from falling off the curb.

Anyway, bringing my cane to work was a scary moment for me. I guess I was "coming out of the closet." I was going to show the world that I had a disability (like limping around that company for the last year wasn't an indicator). My anxiety was through the roof. I could feel my blood pressure spiking. I stood there for a good minute just staring at the cane. I had to talk myself into it. Today was the day. I knew that once I had it out, it couldn't go back— like toothpaste out of the tube. I remember walking into the building. I felt so many eyes on me, not looking at me, but my disability. I felt that I was even less than the half the man I had felt I was. I remember how I would catch people looking at my cane and then they would make eye contact with me, pretending they weren't staring at my cane. I equated it with a guy trying not to look at a woman's cleavage – so smooth. This transition was made tolerable only because of the people of the Production Floor. They know me well enough, and we are close enough that they are honest with me, come rain or shine. They were quick to say, "It's about time." I guess they got tired of my laboring around.

I don't know where this would fit, but I like the fact that I can pick up a 'Side Note' and it puts me right back in the mood I was in when I wrote it and I can talk about it.

[Side Note 08/22/16] You ever have one of those really bad days where you just hate being alive? Here I am at the "happiest place on earth" (Disneyland) and I'm as sad as can be. I couldn't stay too long in the park with Liam because I started to overheat and had to come back to the room. Later, "the princess" saw me fall in the hallway because I couldn't pick my feet up high enough. I hate my M.S. It owned me today. This was a really low point in my life, but I picked myself up and kept moving.

Even when I'm feeling weak, like there's nothing left, I somehow find the strength to keep going. I find a way to finish my mission for the day. I truly believe that the Army prepared me for this life. I soldier on. "I fight the good fight, even on the bad days."[3] (Another line from Talib Kweli – *Push Thru*). How could I not believe in the fact that everything happens for a reason or the idea that my life has been predestined? I'm not sure, but I'm thankful for the strength to fight this. As I've said before, I'm not naïve enough to believe that I could fight my M.S. I would be fighting a losing battle.

No, I fight to finish my day. I fight to complete my mission. I fight the voice that says it's okay to give up because I got the best excuse and reason to stop fighting. Nobody could blame me, because they couldn't see themselves in my shoes. This is why I find pride in seeing the ones that fight when they have every excuse not to. I get strength from the examples they put forth. We are an army of one. We can only fight this kind of fight on our own because it lies within us.

> [Side Note 11/23/18] I hold Nicole in high regard and it just dawned on me why. When I was rebuilding myself because of my identity issues, I had to do it alone. It was hard and lonely. To rebuild this time around, I realize I'm not alone. I have a mentor. I have an example of the best who's ever done

it right here in front of me. I have someone to talk to. I don't reach out to talk to her, but that's on me. She set me on my path to accepting this "new me" and finding my new strength. I just realized this. **_Wow!_**

Chapter 7
Where Do We Go From Here?

That is a good question. I added this chapter because I felt a need for closure, but the truth is I do not know what that is. Outside of death, I don't know what closure looks like. I just keep moving. I want to say that is the key. No matter what obstacle is in my way, no matter what life throws at me, I have to keep moving.

I write this not so much as a testimonial, but to convince myself to keep moving. Giving up is not an option. There have been numerous times that I've had the opportunity to use an excuse and people would understand, thinking, "I'm impressed that he lasted that long." Or "I don't think I could have done it." But I didn't use it.

I want to give up. I want to stop struggling. I want to stop having anxiety issues just from needing to walk. I want to not have the fear of drinking a beverage and not being able to make it to a bathroom. I want to give in and let my M.S. consume me, but I can't. I have responsibilities to my family. They are more important than I.

I guess that's the lesson here: While you are young and single, make the most of your life. Do it all, and live. Regret nothing. Once you settle down and get that family, you need to take the backseat and do whatever has to be done to support them. That means to be there for them mentally, physically, emotionally, financially, *et cetera*. When they look at you, let them feel the fact that you've got them. No matter how much it hurts, how much it takes away from you or instills fear in you, keep moving to be what they want and need.

I'm wondering if this was what was lacking in Robert. From what I remember growing up, I couldn't see him taking a backseat to anyone or anything. He loved the limelight too much, so he kept it shining on himself. With that being said, this is a two-part lesson. Keep moving to do what needs to be done. I like that lesson better because it has purpose. Moving to get nowhere is pointless.

> [Side Note - I had an epiphany while you were on your trip to New York with your mother. I realized that I don't like being alone. It's depressing and sad. I didn't have purpose; I didn't have you. I realized that all my talk of wanting to die would put you

in my shoes. I realized that I would not want you to feel the loneliness I felt. I'm sorry for my selfishness. I now have to catch myself and remind myself that I would not want to bestow that kind of sadness on you. It is debilitating.]

While you were in New York, I had to make a list of things to do for each day. When the tasks were done for the day, I got ready for bed. In almost every case, I was in bed by 8:30. It was sad. I was reminded of the dichotomy of existence. We are born to die. While there is life, we can choose to take advantage of it, or we can just wait to die. Before I started having mobility issues, I moved to live. After I was so quick to say that I've lived a good life, that I wouldn't trade it for anything, then I stopped living and waited to die. I'm sorry for that mind-set. It was a disservice to you.

I had another epiphany the other day. How many epiphanies can you have in a lifetime? How many times have I used 'epiphany' while writing this? I'm going to have to do a word search to see. I think the epiphanies happen because my mind trails off in thought way too much. Anyway…I have come to realize why I came up with an ending of "Where Do We Go From Here?" I realized that I asked for 10 years because I wanted to get you to 16 years old, even if my calculations were off.

While I'm writing this, I'm trying to calculate how old you will be when 10 is up. There's that trailing off. Anyway…I realized that my vision was for your maturation, but I never thought of where I would be.

I realized that I need to get it right so you will not be stuck with what's left behind. I need to get my finances right. I do not want you to be stuck with having to cover my debts. Your grandma says that she's going to start playing the lottery again. If she wins, she said that she would "help a brother out." This made me smile because I don't hold any stock in the fact that she will win, but I like the idea that she has hope of winning and helping me out.

I need to get this right. I need to have a plan to get this right. I need to develop the next step. I need a Plan B.

So, I wrote this, and I don't know why, but I want to add it as a lesson, even if it's just a side note.

> [Side Note - Do you know what it's like to lie in bed, not wanting to get up? Then you get hit with the fear of that day when you're not able to get up. So, you fight the fear and get up. Time to grind. Every day we fight. I won't win the war, but I'll win today's battle.]

The lesson here is to keep fighting, at all costs. We don't give up. Fear is not physical, so it can't physically stop you. Only you, or physical restraints, can do that. I hope I've shown you that with each day I continue to keep going despite my M.S., I know you can't see the fear, frustration, and anxiety that shrouds my day. But it's always there, with every step. I don't want to – I have to. This is the job. This is what's expected. I have responsibilities that are bigger than my fears, frustrations, and anxiety. I man-up and do what needs to be done to support the family.

Another lesson I want to pass on is: Don't be afraid to fail. It shows that you tried. It is true that those who never try never fail, but they also don't grow. This is what I consider being mediocre. I've failed quite a few times in my life. I wouldn't say "a lot." but it was more than once. I would like to think I learned from those failures, and that I've gained strength and wisdom in the process. Hopefully, you have benefited from this.

> [Side Note 11/04/18]: You're going to fall sometimes and that's okay. You can't reach new heights if you do not attempt to fly. Also, when you fly, there's a chance that you may fall. The strength of a person's character is based on what they do next.

Yeah, I've physically fallen many times, sometimes in one day, and not metaphorically. Thanks to my M.S., and yes, I developed anxiety from having to perform such menial tasks as walking or climbing a ladder. But with each fall, I've gotten back up, knowing I'll fall again. As long as I'm close to a wall, furniture, or object that I can use my upper body strength to get to my feet, I can reset and go again. If there's nothing within reach, then I crawl for the nearest thing. I've had people try to help me up, but I'm heavier than I look. With each fall, I was a little smarter about why I fell. This wisdom has made me more focused and not so easily distracted. Each bruise has made me more thankful that I didn't break anything. Each scrape made me manage my time better so I wouldn't be in such a rush. Isn't that the thought process of the quintessential man?

[Side Note 11/24/18] My fight was never against the disease. That's a fight I can't win. The fight was against myself. Against wanting to give up. Against wanting to stop fighting. Against wanting to stop being "strong." The fight was against the day. Today I fight to continue. Today I fight for another day. In this fight, we are all soldiers. It's not about a uniform or the training that I received from the Army. It's about the will to fight. Today we are soldiers fighting the battle. Today we fight to carry on until the next. We may lose the war, but not today.

Keep in mind that you can accomplish anything in life with the right resources, and that starts with those who support you. After spending a few years on my own, rebuilding me, I began to surround myself with people who supported me, believed in me, influenced me, *et cetera*. First and foremost is your grandma. She has been there for me throughout. I always use a house as an analogy for defining who and what we are as people. Some use onions with layers (Shrek reference). Some use puzzles or mazes. I like houses. Every house needs a sound foundation. Your grandma is the bedrock my foundation sits on. I say that because she is my alpha and omega. Without her, there would be no me.

I've had to repair my foundation a few times in my life and rebuild the house that sits on it. Let's just focus on the house I've built since your conception. It is by far the strongest, most elegant, *et cetera*. My support group made that possible. This starts with your mom. I've always equated myself with crude oil, and she refines me. With her, I'm Premium Grade. High octane!

Even though we don't talk that often and it's been years since I've seen him, I would have been deprived to not have Marc in my corner. He is my financial guy and best friend. He was my best friend before he ever thought about going to college, but he was always about money. As a kid, if he loaned you 50¢, he would want 75¢ as payback. From childhood, after the Army, and through marriage, he has been my first call, outside of Mom and Bobbie. Things changed after D-day, but that's a different story.

Then there was Nicole, my unknowing shepherd who enlightened me on the fact that I have a disability and that I need to accept that fact and continue to live my best life. This would explain why I'm not "disabled;" I just have a disability. Marinate on that.

My other support contacts came and went all by mishap, but they left a lasting impression. It all began when I went hunting with Mike and Tom. This was my new hobby and I loved it. I don't think I've ever had a hobby before this, other than collecting comic books. I spent a lot of money on a rifle and scope. I went to the range to make sure my shot was on point. Oh, how I love the smell of gunsmoke. It brought back memories of my Army days.

On our first trip out, I must have fallen 30 times. It got so bad that I got some deep scratches in the stock of my rifle, so Tom offered to carry it for me. After this little incident, I decided to see a physical therapist because I knew my right leg was smaller than the left and I needed to get it built up. Little did I know then what the cause was.

I met Austin at the Premier Physical Therapy place. He was young and very excited to get me right. I really enjoyed that facility and the aides who worked with me. Now, during all this time, everything I said about me getting diagnosed was going on.

After D-day, I told Austin about the real cause of my issue. He didn't skip a beat. The cool thing was that he researched the disease in his free time and gave me pointers to help me. The best advice he gave me was, if I ever get overheated, I should put ice packs under my arms and at the base of my neck to cool down fast. He was also the one who showed me how to walk with a cane. This was helpful for the trip to Disneyland that summer.

Austin ended up moving to the Carson City branch of Premier Physical Therapy and I wasn't about to make that drive. I ended up getting passed around to different therapists until I stopped going to that facility. I found another physical therapist who had a private practice. It's amazing how so few physical therapists specialize in caring for those with M.S. In any case, the practice didn't last, and he ended up going to work for one of the bigger centers.

Now would be a good time to explain the permanent symptom that I have because of my M.S. It's referred to as "drop-foot" or "foot-drop." My right leg doesn't flex the foot upward as it normally would. It's like the foot is hanging down. If I don't pay attention to how I walk, my foot drags and catches on things, like the floor, rugs, cables, *et cetera*. My biggest fear is stepping over a cable on the carpet. It makes me nervous, like a cat in a room full of rocking chairs. I nicknamed my left leg "dead leg" because it feels like I am dragging a dead body around. I contemplated having it amputated; then I wouldn't have expectations of it working.

If I lose focus for one second I will fall. Before the cane, I fell a lot. The worst was when I was with you. I knew it embarrassed you so much and it broke my heart whenever it happened, especially out in public. It got so bad that I started having anxiety issues whenever I was out in public. I held your hand a lot and I never fell while holding your hand. Even after I started walking with a cane, there were times when I fell. Whenever I was in a rush, trying to walk and talk at the same time, or toward the end of the workday when I was exhausted, the chances of me falling would increase. One day, when I was attending a class on the UNR campus, my anxiety got so high I froze and couldn't take a step. It was a Saturday and there was some kind of function on campus. I was walking back to the parking garage to go home and there were a lot of people in my path. I stood next to a rail trying to move and couldn't. After about five minutes, my soldier-mentality kicked in. In my head, I yelled at myself to stop being a baby (clean version). *Are you going to stand here and cry until someone helps you cross the street?* (inner voice) I paced out my next steps in an Army cadence. Left, right, left, right. I made it back to my truck and sat there until the shaking stopped. There are times as I'm walking through the backyard to clean up after the dog, when I thought that if this was being recorded on video, it would make for a good thriller. The viewer is left in suspense as I attempt to navigate unstable ground on a hunt for Daisy's presents. I've fallen more times in my backyard than I can count. The "fun" part is when I have to contort my body to keep from landing in dog shit . . . but I digress. You see, I'd been taking a break since my last physical therapist and it was taking a toll on me.

    I figured I'd try something new, since the years of physical therapy didn't get me anywhere. It was a toss-up between Pilates and yoga. I knew that I wasn't going to simply join a class. As bad as my mobility was, it wouldn't go well. I looked for someone who specialized in M.S. patients and offered private instruction. I came up empty so I started reading bios of the instructors to see if I could get lucky. I did, with one private practice physical therapist. I came across Miss Julia. She offered private yoga therapy sessions at her studio called Mindful Care Yoga.

Miss Julia had me fill out a survey so she would know what I was looking for and what my expectations were. Our first session was mostly an interview. Miss Julia wears her heart on her sleeve. When I told her my M.S. story, I could see the sympathy in her eyes. She was honest with me in telling me that she's never dealt with anyone with M.S. and that she would be journeying into the unknown, but she was willing to give it a try.

The funny thing is that all the physical therapists that I had seen up to that point had never dealt with someone with M.S. either. I guess we are a rare breed. With Miss Julia, I took a leap of faith because she exposed her weakness, but it was her desire to understand that won me over. I told her that you can't make an omelet without breaking some eggs, so we got cracking. I've always been bothered by the fact that my dead leg had atrophied to the point that it was noticeable. When Miss Julia felt it for the first time, she described it as "cold and clammy." So she focused on that. She was the only one to actually focus on what I saw as a problem. I had made the right decision.

I think it was our second session when she had me focus on getting a particular muscle in my leg to respond. I would feel the muscle in my good leg to see which one I wanted to focus on, and then I would try to get the dead leg to respond. The damn thing worked! Something so simple, but it worked. I had told Miss Julia about my desire to possibly have my leg amputated; she wasn't too happy with that idea. She also didn't like me calling it a "dead leg."

The simplest idea of focusing on the muscle to move instead of relying on muscle memory made a difference. I guess the mindfulness of this practice showed promise. See what I did there… mindful. Anyway, this was a groundbreaking breakthrough. Miss Julia was so happy she shed a tear. When I said I wouldn't cry, she told me that the studio was a safe place to cry. I was happy and sad at the same time. I was happy for the movement, but I was also sad that it was my stubborn behavior that had got me to this point. I was so against everything the Army forced me to do that I wouldn't do it anymore. This included staying in shape with exercise, especially running, but that's another story.

After a few sessions, I stopped referring to my right leg as "my dead leg." I decided to call it

Lazarus[6] because she brought it back to life. Keeping with the biblical theme, I call my left leg Sampson. She refers to it as "Show off." You would think that our focus would only be on Lazarus, but that wasn't the case. She also worked with me on breath control. When we first started our sessions, Miss Julia told me, "Breath is life." That stuck with me. I realized that through breath control, I could meditate, reduce my stress, and even stop hiccups. She also introduced me to the Six-positions-of-the-spine exercise.

I'll tell you why the Six-positions-of-the-spine was a huge gift for me, but I have to give you some backstory. After my M.S. kicked into high gear, I would find myself struggling to make it to the bathroom in the morning after waking up. I knew it was three steps to the bathroom entry. The ability, or lack thereof, to make those three steps would determine how my day was going to go. There were also days when I couldn't stand on my feet long enough to take a step. I'd just fall back in bed and email work that I was taking a sick day. Some mornings I would lie in bed wondering if my body was going to fail me. The Six-positions-of-the-spine exercise changed the game for me. I'd get up, sit at the edge of the bed, work through the six positions, get to my feet, and walk to the bathroom to take my shower and start my day. It was as simple as that.

What I want to drive home, is that Miss Julia didn't just work on my physical problem. She worked on my overall well-being. The anxiety I'd get whenever I needed to walk somewhere was reduced a lot. Don't get me wrong, I was still falling, even with the cane, but my fear was reduced and I was more confident about moving around. Once I started using the forearm crutches, the anxiety was all but gone.

I love the time she gives me and the enthusiasm she has when trying new things with me. Some are uncomfortable, but I give it a try because I trust her wholeheartedly. Within six months, she has made more progress than the six years I spent in physical therapy. She's given me hope, and that's propelled me to exercise more, improve my dietary habits, and finish this book. She has given me a glimpse beyond the ten-year request. I won't go as far as saying that she saved my life, but she did bring light to my dark days.

Chapter 8
Fight the Power

When I started writing this book, the only thing that I had to worry about was M.S. dropping the other shoe on me. It always seems to be hanging around, even to the point that your mother and I were looking into getting more life insurance for ourselves outside of our jobs. Keep this in mind as I'll bring it up again. So, just when I'm thinking that just as things are starting to look up for me, 2020 hits us with the CoronaVirus – COVID 19.

I'm not sure that surreal would be the right word, but I'll use it anyway. The number of deaths that the pandemic brought was surreal in the sense that it didn't take much to put someone in the I.C.U. on a ventilator, and once they were there, their chances of survival weren't too good. Here I was with a compromised immune system, thanks to my M.S. medication. Your mom put me on lockdown. I wasn't allowed to go shopping at COSTCO anymore. The governor put out restrictions for the state for all companies that weren't considered essential. These nonessential companies had to close. Lucky me (sarcasm), my company was essential, which meant I had to go to work. What with all the individuals who lost their jobs, I'm thankful. Luckily, everyone in the house was either considered "essential workers" or were able to work from home, like your mom.

The pandemic was something that I have never experienced in my life, but then my life is full of firsts. To this I adapted, like everybody else. Miss Julia and I had to switch to yoga sessions online. It wasn't the same because I could cheat on some of my exercises and the video didn't show it. I know, I was just cheating myself. I was thankful to be able to Zoom my sessions because even at half-effort, it was better than me being on my own.

Losing my live yoga sessions was the one negative I could point to, when it came to the pandemic. I know that someone would point out all the deaths, but that didn't affect me any more than the death that normally occurs in the world, except knowing that the magnitude was far greater than normal.

I guess the other negative was more of an obvious observation, like being told that I'm old. This observation came as we were looking to get life insurance. Your mom was able to get a policy with no issues. For me, the poor agent didn't really know how to tell me that he couldn't find a company that was willing to insure me – at any cost. Think about that, I was such a high risk that nobody would take that chance. I felt like I was being told that COVID was going to kill me – it wasn't a matter of *if*, but *when*.

I would say they were right because I do have it written in my living will that I am not to be placed on any type of machine to sustain my life. I wouldn't want to risk being in a vegetative state or losing one iota of my cognitive capacity. This is how I make my money. I would rather die. Literally. I can handle losing physical abilities, but to not be in my right mind would be unbearable. I digress.

I loved the fact that we could get almost anything delivered to the house. I loved the fact that I didn't have to shop. Even when your mother went to Seattle, I was able to have the grocery store shop for me and then put it in the car. Restaurants had curbside delivery. OMG! For a person with a mobility problem, this was heaven.

It wasn't all love and deliveries though. As I said, I was considered essential because of the job. I didn't want to be at work because their policy for dealing with COVID was shady and suspect. All the while, I began to step into the comfort of my disability. Getting up and down the stairs became too much of a chore for me, so I asked if I could get a desk on the first floor. They ended up putting me in a cubicle two buildings away from the production floor. I was in isolation in that building. None of the people around me worked in manufacturing. I ordered everything that I would need to remain comfortable in my new surroundings. I bought a red stapler. (Pop culture reference.)

Out of nowhere, I had heard that some individuals from another building were volunteering to set up a new building to build ventilators. At the time I was feeling so worthless trapped at home and only being allowed to go to work. So many people were dying in hospitals waiting for ventilators. I contacted the Vice President of R&D Engineering and offered my services to the project in whatever capacity they could use them. He accepted and I was in. They were in a different location, and this was for the medical division of the company. I knew of this division, but I've always been a part of the manufacturing side of things.

We had to build this factory from the ground up. They bought a warehouse with nothing in it and within three weeks we had a manufacturing facility. This would not have been possible if not for GM. Yes, General Motors was teaming up with us to make this work. I didn't realize how big this was until I saw a news article about the contract with FEMA worth a half-billion dollars.

GM flew in their best from Detroit, and they didn't disappoint. They moved at a pace that I hadn't been around since my days at Arrow Electronics. I was loving every minute of it. I was working long days and weekends. I was trying to be an asset. I want to think that I was, and I met some really smart and gung-ho people. I was a little sad when the project was complete and handed over to Operations. The one really cool thing that I got out of it was a video of news footage of what we had done and it showed me giving a demonstration of some environmental chambers that I had installed and programmed. I was able to email it to the family. Your grandma was so proud. I was doing my part to fight this war against COVID. I was a soldier.

Chapter 9
Evolutionary Change

The two constants in my life that I welcome with open arms are change and music. Change because this is what the Army taught me. The Army taught me how to adapt to whatever condition I found myself in. This is a valuable item in my toolbox because it keeps me prepared for the worst. Yeah, it took a therapist to get me to realize that I had this tool. Even though it is useful, it is a double-edged sword. I can adapt to new situations because I do not develop strong ties to many things. I lose friends, coworkers, neighbors, and family. I recover from it all. Music is the other constant because it has always been there throughout my life.

When I was a child, Grannie played her gospel records. Brad and I would put tissue paper under the records in order to scratch, which was big during the time, to be a D.J. Your grandma loved listening to Kenny Rogers. "You gotta know when to hold 'em. Know when to fold 'em. Know when to walk away. Know when to run."

When I went through basic training, we got hype to Guns & Roses "Welcome To The Jungle." Bobby McFerrin's "Don't Worry Be Happy" was also popular at the time, but that song would provoke a lot of hostility. In Germany, I listened to anything with a lot of bass in it. I had bought these Cerwin Vega speakers and I just wanted to shake stuff up. Yeah, I was that obnoxious guy. I remember being on guard duty at nights, freezing on some hilltop in Germany, and I would sing Luther Vandross' "A House Is Not A Home" as I walked my post. It's funny that when I think of this song, I think of Aunt Nina. I can't tell you why.

Being back in Fort Hood expanded my music exposure, not necessarily for the good. The effect of music connecting events in my life allowed a lot of negativities to linger. I wasn't prepared for dealing with those emotions, so I buried them.

Being with Marc, *getting one in* on the Sega Genesis, allowed me some moments for exorcizing the negative emotions. This was a safe place as long as I didn't spill any beer or mess up on a play. Marc and I played a lot of oldies-but-goodies. Stevie Wonder was his favorite, by far. Al Green was a frequently played artist. Then there was Prince, "Sexy M.F.." Marc's old college roommate would come through talking about the Wu-tang Clan. This got me hooked on East Coast hip-hop.

After moving to Phoenix and being alone, I became severely depressed and listened to too much music which exacerbated my mood. After rebuilding me and moving to Reno, I started using music to set my mood. With the evolution of music devices, my use of music evolved. I grew up listening to 8-track tapes, vinyl records, and cassette tapes. I listened to the cassette tapes on a Walkman. In the Army, we mainly listened to CDs. I had so many Disc-man players. Then came digital music and the iPods, Zune, MP3 players, etc. Then, enter the smartphone. The point of these changes was to make music accessible and mobile.

As a civilian, before I met your mother, I traveled a lot for Arrow Electronics. I would listen to my music on planes, in airports, in hotel rooms, on trains, and just about everywhere I went. I used music to occupy my time and mediate my mood. While studying, I listened to classical music in the beginning because I had read an article in *Psychology Today* that said listening to classical music helped your memory, which made studying easier. As I grew older, I realized that classical music wasn't the thing that made studying easier. It was the fact that it didn't have vocals. It had to be instrumental music that allowed me to focus. If there were vocals in the music, the lyrics would draw my attention. The instrumental music becomes background sound that blocks out distractions. I still listen to classical music when I study, but when I really need to concentrate, I put on some smooth jazz. My favorite album to study to is Thelonious Monk's "Straight No Chaser." I originally got this when I was in England on a trip for Arrow. I was taking online classes to get my electrical engineering degree to get my pay up. Now I use internet radio stations on my phone when I need to study, but I still put on Thelonious when I need to really pay attention.

The two songs that come to mind when I think of your mother are by Prince. The first is "Adore." The lyrics on this one set my mood and bring a smile to my face every time I hear it. The start of the song sums up a lot: "Love is 2 weak 2 define Just what U mean 2 me."[13] This is why I adore your mother. "Until the end of time, I'll be there for you."[13] This is so true because your mother is the dawn to my new life, and she will be the sunset on that life. Too deep? Prince music will do that to you. The second Prince song is "Insatiable."[14] I actually had to look up the definition of insatiable.

In your first year, I took pictures of you almost every day that I was in the country. The only way that I wasn't home was when I was traveling for work. I had to make that money because I had an extra mouth to feed. Anyway, I made a video/slideshow of your pictures with music. These songs were what I tied to how I felt about your place in my life. The first one, I titled "The Beginning." It starts with a video that I took of you at 3:00 o'clock in the morning after the nurses cleaned and bundled you up. I called Marc and told him that you were here and then I videoed you. Then there's a slideshow of videos with Roberta Flack's "The First Time Ever I Saw Your Face."[5] I felt the earth move in my hands.

The next video I did was photos of your ultrasounds. The baby's life begins when it is acknowledged. This video had Sade's "Kiss of Life"[15] playing because "You wrap me up in the color of love."[15] Music video #1 is to Patti Labelle's "My Love, Sweet Love."[11] To this day, when I hear this song, it warms my heart and makes me smile because I think of you. You are my heart, and my heart is yours. Music video #2 has Luther Vandross' "Here and Now."[18] Check the lyrics and you'll understand. "When I look in your eyes and I know what you mean to me."[18] Music video #3 is to Chaka Khan's "My Funny Valentine." The line that gets me with this one is "You make me smile with my heart"[10]. Music video #4, the final video, sums it all up. It's set to Prince's "Baby, I'm A Star."[12] They might not know it now, but you *are* a star.

That music has changed, defined, linked, chronicled, and aided my life cannot be overstated. Music is the way I navigate my life. Any significant part of my life has a song tied to it. In some cases, many songs. I'm hoping that as I grow older and my memory fades, I can put on the playlist of my life and reminisce. If I am capable of accomplishing this task, I'm going to be alright.

Just as my exposure to music evolved and showed purpose, so have my educational endeavors. If it weren't for the fact that I had a hard time spelling while I was in the Army, or the girl embarrassing me about not knowing what M.B.A. meant, or Arrow Electronics having me get a degree from an unaccredited college, I would not have expanded my knowledge of the educational apparatus and all its nuances. I would not have figured out that you could get into any public college as a transfer student if you took the required credits at the affiliated community college. I would not have figured out that you can get into college with a G.E.D., without graduating high school. I figured out a lot of seemingly simple things, just through observation and research. I have moved to an understanding of the simplicities of our society, human nature, and motivations. I figured out more than that, but these are pretty big. In the spirit of W.E.B. Du Bois, "I've peered behind the veil."

In doing so, I've expanded my interest in human behavior to include sociological aspects that affect it. This is the current evolutionary change that I'm experiencing. The weird part is that it all comes full circle with "Fighting The Good Fight." In the words of Tavis Smiley, "I'll unpack that for you." Growing up as a lower-income child in a single-mother household has influenced my life. It drove me to the military. The sad part of reality is that when you are black and brought up in a community of lower socioeconomic status, the odds are against you succeeding. There are two main ways out that seem readily available, one of which is positive, and the other negative, but seemingly unavoidable. It's either through the military complex or the criminal justice complex. I chose the latter. It's not that anyone chooses to be in the criminal justice system, but if you are a black male with no legitimate goals or ambitions, the criminal justice apparatus comes calling.

I never really knew the power of an education until I began to obtain one. The truth is that you never really stop once you've started. It just evolves. This is Grannie's legacy to me. I realize that there is another direction to go in besides the military and jail –education, and it's got a higher probability of success than the other two. This has given drive to my mission statement. I want to shine the light on education for those who were convinced that, with a high school diploma or as a high school dropout, all they would be able to accomplish is to (hopefully) be a manager of a supermarket or a McDonalds. Not that there's anything wrong with that, but that needs to be an option, not an inevitability.

Where am I going with this? I realized that if I set you on the path of education, then all I have to do is facilitate your journey to the best of my ability and means. If I accomplish this, your intellect will rival anyone's. Yeah, I'm sure genetics could have played some part in it, but it was mostly the societal elements in your upbringing that positioned you to be amazing. Yes, we had to move to another neighborhood to be zoned for a better public school, and money was spent to get you some good tutors when you needed them, but that put you in the 99th percentile for education. At the end of the day, your foundation is based on the simplicity of reading, writing, and mathematics. If you can read, you can understand anything. If there's a word you don't understand, there's a dictionary to define it for you. I have a Webster's Dictionary app on my smartphone that I use almost every day. I'm not ashamed of that and my vocabulary is extensive, if I do say so myself.

A lot of people are afraid of math, but the truth is if you can add, subtract, multiply, and divide, the rest is just different rules and formulas that you learn through reading. This was always the basis that I applied to you kids as you grew up. With you, though, since I was making some good money, we were able to put your practice on steroids. I was able to put you in the math club. I was able to get you tutoring in the Learning Center, which got you into one of the finest public schools in the nation, luckily, in our town. There is no secret to it, there is only a veil of secrecy.

Chapter 10
Final Words (for now)

So why did I write this? Well, I wanted you to know me. I wanted you to understand what makes me tick. I didn't know much about your grandpa. Most of what I did know came from other sources, not the man himself. Robert never talked to me about his life. It seemed as if everyone in Midland knew him and I didn't. For some reason, I think that had I gotten to know him, it would have given me structure for my life. You know that saying, "You don't know where you are going until you know where you've been." I'm not saying that you will ever experience many of the things that I have. You were not brought up in poverty. Hopefully, you will not join the Army. Most importantly, I pray you will not experience a debilitating condition as I have. Most important, though, I am here for you.

My life, or just life in general, is full of ups and downs, twists, and turns. The obstacles that get in your way cannot stop you. They just make your journey a little longer, a little tougher. The hardships that you face don't need to define who you are. I've given you a glimpse into who I have been. So, when you see me now, you see that there has been an evolutionary change. The definition that I like for evolution is: a process of continuous change from a lower, simpler, or worse, to a higher, more complex, or better state.

With everything that I've endured over the span of my life, I should have died a few times, or I could have taken a few bad turns – and I probably did along the way– but I'm here. This is why I say that I'm blessed. I remember a discussion you and I had about religion and going to church because our neighbors went to church. You made the comment that you were an atheist and I told you that you weren't. I went on to explain that I am agnostic because I don't have the hard facts. The definition that suits me is "a person who holds the view that any ultimate reality (such as God) is unknown and probably unknowable," (Merriam-Webster). I told you that it was impossible for me to be an atheist because that wasn't how I was raised and I could not disrespect Grannie like that. She died believing in Jesus and that heaven awaited her. After writing this book, I recognize the blessings that were there all this time. From finding help, finding my true self, finding your mom, to having you. I'd be a fool to think that God didn't have a hand in this. Sure, I have M.S. and that sucks, but I would just consider it a penance for a life that I haphazardly placed in jeopardy so many times. A lot of time has passed since we had that discussion. In that time two things happened; you got older and I got wiser. I'm wise enough to know that I cannot tell you what you can and cannot be. I didn't like it when it was forced on me as a kid. You are smart enough to make your own decisions based on your experiences and the effects that they have on you. That being said, I recant the idea that I'm agnostic. When I prayed to God to give me ten years to get my affairs in order, He showed up and showed out. I got my ten and I'm still going. Not only am I going, but I'm flourishing. I'm taking chances that I would not have taken before and it's gratifying. I told Mom that after reaching the ten-year agreement, I would recognize my blessings and just say "Thank you."

What I want you to understand is that you have a strength in you to overcome any obstacles that get in your way. I've spoken to you many times about establishing generational wealth. When I speak of "wealth," it's not just monetary. I'm talking about the stories, the experiences, the lessons learned. I'm talking about the struggle. There is wealth in all of it, just like "Every cloud has a silver lining." I've heard this said, but I've never seen it. I've also heard that there are blessings in every lesson, you just need to recognize them.

It's not about the knowledge gained, but the wisdom you pass on. All that I've done since your conception, I've done for you and because of you. Your life has been my greatest love and my greatest fear. My love for you is truly unconditional. My fear is in failing to be someone you can be proud of. There were moments when I was going to go get milk (Simpson's reference to Nelson's father). I faced my fears. I stepped up to the challenge.

Writing this book has been difficult. A lot of old wounds have been reopened. A lot of hurtful and haunting memories have resurfaced, but I'm stronger than I was back then. I have purpose; that purpose is you. With that as my shield, nothing will stop me.

> [Side Note 08/21/19] (I had to add this in because I want you to understand how much this day meant to me.) Today was Orientation Day for your first year in the Davidson Academy and we had to get you a UNR Campus ID (Wolfcard). Normally I'd have an anxiety attack knowing that I would have to walk from the parking garage to the Student Union. Let's be honest, I get anxious walking from my bed to

the kitchen. I didn't get the anxiety of having to walk today. Hell, I could have run to the parking spot kiosk. In fact, I left my cane and then came back to get it, with no problem. "My 13-year-old just got an I.D. with the university!" To say that I was walking on clouds as the proudest dad ever would be an understatement.

If I could do my life all over again, I wouldn't change one thing because all things got me here, and I can't think of a better place to be, or a better life.

Not the End.

Epilogue

I had not considered writing an epilogue for this book, but two things happened in May that wouldn't allow me not to acknowledge and put it here. I have them as side notes because, after they happened, I was "shook" and needed to write down what I was feeling.

[Side Note 05/12/22] I haven't written a "Side Note" in a long while, but after last night's conversation with you, I had to get this off my chest. It's not often that I get "gut-punched" bad enough that it makes me rethink the decisions I've made in order to move forward with my life. I'm glad that you and I have an unfiltered comfort of communication, but it can be brutal at times. When you told me that you got a notice about my Instagram account, and it was *cringe*, my heart fell into my stomach. You made your point when you warned me to not sell anything online. I was taken aback by the lack of support, but I think you sensed that when you tried to placate me with the "you do you" statement.

Although our conversation didn't go as I had hoped, it did open my eyes to a few things. I am grateful you can be honest with me. You would be the one I go to for the hard, real truth, not the watered-down version. Your mother gives the hard truth, but reins it in to keep from hurting someone's feelings.

As you commented on my listening to other people's issues, I recognized that you were protecting me. At first, I was under the assumption that you were just embarrassed, and you probably are, but I sensed some worry in your voice, and it was for my well-being.

Most importantly, and probably the thing that got me shook, was you driving at why I'm doing this. This got me to really think about this decision. I say that it's my retirement plan – the way I am going to be making any money to survive when I can no longer handle the workload of an engineer. This is a conundrum.

From the heart, I just want to be a resource, an ear, a conscience, a *whatever,* that someone would need to get over the hump or past the obstacle that's holding them up. I just want to be a guide for the lost. I want to live in the mantra I chose: *If I can help somebody as I pass along; if I can cheer somebody with a word or song; if I can show somebody he's (she's) traveling wrong; then my living will not be in vain.* - Martin Luther King Jr.

With what you've presented to me, I'm shook, but I must move forward. I've taken in everything you said – and didn't say. That's probably why it stings, but I'll figure out how to adapt and evolve into someone you can be proud of. This was my mindset, and then it hit me. Everything I experienced with my conversation with you made me realize that this is what I would have done. You have always told me that you are my legacy. That statement continues to be true.

[Side Note 05/22/22] I guess you can say it broke my heart to have your mother tell me that my life is not interesting enough to be a book. I had to look for Tavis Smiley's essay in which he said, "Never mind the naysayers to get inspiration to understanding that I'm doing what I feel is right for me." He said, "Do you?" I guess this is why this is going to be the foreword in my book. In the beginning, I wrote "I'm not sure why I am doing this," until I focused on the fact that I'm doing this for you. My mission statement is my mantra.

What makes me happy is making others happy. I guess that's me doing this in love. So, I'll never mind the naysayers, and continue to do what I do because it's in love.

The culmination of both acts caused me to pause. I had to rethink my efforts. Thus Dante S. Wendell was born. Dante from the times we were in the clubs when I was in the Army, and in Austin with Marc. You needed a fake name in case things went wrong. Mine was Dante. Wendell from "Mr. Wendal" by *Arrested Development* because I wish to be "Free to be without the worries." 'S' for StreetCornerCounselor.

Acknowledgement

I told myself I was going to stop writing or this thing will never get done, but I got moved by something today that I need to acknowledge. But where to put it? Hence this section. But if I'm going to do this section, I've got to start off right. I must give thanks to the Most High and all my angels that have shed light on my path. I am truly blessed. For those still in the flesh, who have given a prayer for me, thank you. To my mother, all that I am is because of you. I hope you are proud. To the ones in my support group, knowingly or not, thank you for holding me up and allowing me to lean on you. To Miss Julia, the drill sergeant and savior, thank you for giving me my breath and hope. To Tavis Smiley and the crew at KBLA 1580 (I have the app), thank you for the entertainment, education, and empowerment. Today I heard the interview with Master P. in the studio. "Y'all were dropping bars and scriptures." What I walked away from it was this, "A loss is a lesson" (Master P.) and Matthew 23; 11: "But who is greatest among you shall be your servant." I've lost a lot to M.S., but I've also gained a lot and I am ready to serve.

My Playlist

[1] Bambaataa, A. (1982). "Planet Rock." Retrieved from https://open.spotify.com/track/4FupIlegZgvXUuK79qcoKW?si=ad6c469bd1d940d3

[2] Blige, M. (1994). "My Life." Retrieved from https://open.spotify.com/track/7ytES33eLYS9WaZLKqWfYM?si=32bd18286e104960

[3] Curren$y, Reynolds, G., Lamar, K., and Kweli, T. (2013). "Push Thru (**Explicit**)." Retrieved from https://open.spotify.com/track/3WeLxo3f1T6pjfj8Fexz9D?si=d7365e55cc174872

[4] Flack, R. (1973). "Killing Me Softly With His Song." Retrieved from https://open.spotify.com/track/3gsCAGsWr6pUm1Vy7CPPob?si=72ff64ed12804508

[5] Flack, R. (1972). "The First Time Ever I Saw Your Face." Retrieved from

https://open.spotify.com/track/0SxFyA4FqmEQqZVuAlg8lf?si=4c64d9a12e124ce2

[6] Franklin, A. (1972). "Mary, Don't You Weep." Retrieved from

https://open.spotify.com/track/3VZawvF6KNZ0m4MArrhzPJ?si=e345b23269a3473c

[7] Hall, D. and Oates, J. (1980). "Kiss on My List." Retrieved from

https://open.spotify.com/track/7cDzJyC95jtGO9zAeZsWOg?si=cea26c7e12bd407a

[8] Hamilton, A. (2003). "Comin' from Where I'm From." Retrieved from

https://open.spotify.com/track/6UeROtzgj12WLgZx3033G6?si=e36b309f3f994a6a

[9] Jackson, M. (1980). "She's Out of My Life." Retrieved from

https://open.spotify.com/track/6NGsHLZYGVAkXTFr75WWnn?si=6154e06e706f435b

[10] Khan, C. (1995). "My Funny Valentine." Retrieved from

https://open.spotify.com/track/1yaqIxledr7Tpdp5hGU8wf?si=01dc4104680b4e2d

[11] LaBelle, P. (1995). "My Love, Sweet

Love." Retrieved from https://open.spotify.com/track/0w2aeFFUhtTvu5RNgSMkXd?si=28d94264518c4df4

[12] Prince (1984). "Baby I'm a Star." Retrieved from https://open.spotify.com/track/2soBvUQBf5rbMj9HIyhzzK?si=0c5b446ca9ee4f78

[13] Prince (1987). "Adore (**Explicit**)." Retrieved from https://open.spotify.com/track/2xsTC3V51PvY38QK4QNWN0?si=f712a752a97c41db

[14] Prince (1991). "Insatiable." Retrieved from https://open.spotify.com/track/3q4SUOc4upvsrFItSrELsX?si=59e98c4389cd4ecc

[15] Sade (1993). "Kiss of Life." Retrieved from https://open.spotify.com/track/65krtHkaYLPr0mEbjL61UP?si=5f120bdbf1194c5a

[16] The Notorious B.I.G. (1997). "Ten Crack Commandments (**Explicit**)." Retrieved from https://open.spotify.com/track/4xtq6uY0ofikksLWN37pT4?si=9eba224d63f74428

[17] The Temptations (1972). "Papa Was A Rollin' Stone." Retrieved from https://open.spotify.com/track/7MiLmLbwNoyf47xQ4TCVYp?si=39b1c2a3973242c4

[18] Vandross, L. (1989). "Here and Now." Retrieved from https://open.spotify.com/track/042pmCix7CPth3l3X28jl1?si=b49d9422289a4613

About the Author

Michael was born and raised in West Texas. He went on to see the world as a soldier and an engineer before settling down in Reno, Nevada. He is living his best life with his wife, kids, and grandchildren.

www.ingramcontent.com/pod-product-compliance
Lightning Source LLC
Chambersburg PA
CBHW070109080526
44586CB00013B/1244